Easy Paper Crafting With Photos™

Edited by Vicki Blizzard

HOUSE of WHITE BIRCHES
PUBLISHERS SINCE 1947

Easy Paper Crafting With Photos™

EXECUTIVE EDITOR	Vicki Blizzard
EDITOR	Tanya Fox
ART DIRECTOR	Brad Snow
PUBLISHING SERVICES MANAGER	Brenda Gallmeyer
ASSOCIATE EDITOR	Sue Reeves
ASSISTANT ART DIRECTOR	Nick Pierce
COPY SUPERVISOR	Michelle Beck
COPY EDITOR	Mary O'Donnell
TECHNICAL EDITOR	Läna Schurb
PHOTOGRAPHY	Tammy Christian, Don Clark, Matt Owen
PHOTOGRAPHY STYLISTS	Tammy Nussbaum, Tammy Smith
GRAPHIC ARTS SUPERVISOR	Ronda Bechinski
GRAPHIC ARTISTS	Erin Augsburger, Pam Gregory
PRODUCTION ASSISTANTS	Cheryl Kempf, Marj Morgan, Judy Neuenschwander
TECHNICAL ARTISTS	Nicole Gage, Leigh Maley

PUBLISHING DIRECTOR	David J. McKee
MARKETING DIRECTOR	Dan Fink
EDITORIAL DIRECTOR	Gary Richardson

Printed in China
First Printing: 2006
Library of Congress Number: 2005925079

Hard cover:
ISBN-10: 1-59217-082-X
ISBN-13: 978-1-59217-082-1

Soft cover:
ISBN-10: 1-59217-089-7
ISBN-13: 978-1-59217-089-0

1 2 3 4 5 6 7 8 9

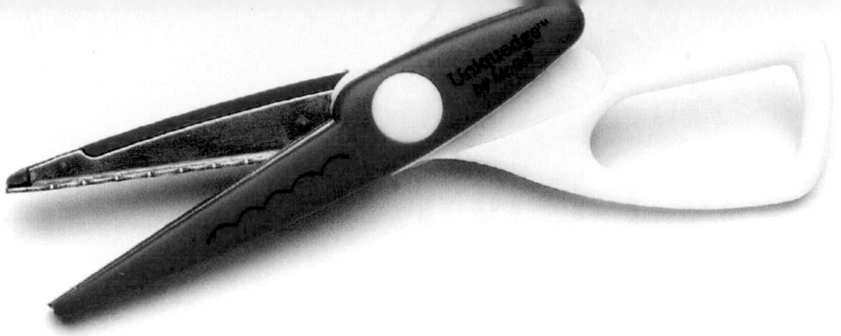

Dear Paper/Photo Crafter,

Taking photos of vacations and special events is something we've all done. Now, the rising popularity of digital cameras makes it easier to record even the day-to-day events in the lives of our families. If you're anything like me, you have boxes and boxes of photos waiting to be put in scrapbooks and albums.

After you've scrapbooked everything you possibly can, though, what do you do with all the extra photos? Most of us can't bear to throw them away—and now you won't have to!

Take a look at the great projects in this book—albums, altered CDs, coasters, cards, frames and so much more. We've even included a few really special scrapbook page layouts that are too pretty to put in albums; you'll want to frame them and hang them on the wall.

With almost 100 unique ideas, you're sure to find the perfect project for your treasured photos.

Warm regards,

Vicki

CONTENTS

Shivers
Michael

Earth laughs in flowers
bloom

blooming memories

CARDS & TAGS

Show someone special how much you care by sending cards and tags embellished with treasured photos.

UNIQUE MEMORY DISPLAYS

Who says scrapbooking is just for album pages? Take memory crafting to new levels by creating interesting photo displays for your home!

FRAMES

Cherished photos deserve to be surrounded by unique, handcrafted photo frames.

PHOTO BOOKS, JOURNALS & ALBUMS

Full of ideas for creating unique albums, this chapter showcases projects that are perfect for holding small collections of photos.

How Do I Love You?

Design by HEATHER D. WHITE

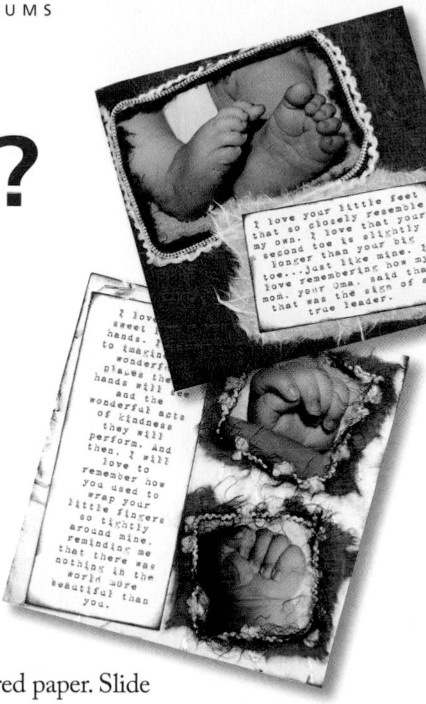

Fill the pages of a handmade album with messages to your sweet new baby.

Project note: *Adhere elements using double-sided tape unless instructed otherwise.*

Cover: Cut red handmade-style paper to cover front of book. Use computer to generate, or hand-print, "I How do I [love] you … Let me count the ways …" on vellum to fit within a strip covering about half of the cover, leaving a blank space at "[love]" for square brads to spell "love." Tear edges of vellum; adhere to right half of red paper. Slide photo partially under vellum; adhere to layout. Tear pieces of black handmade paper to fit in upper right and lower right corners of cover; adhere to layout. Embellish cover corners with silver mini brads and heart eyelet charm. Adhere stickers to square brads to spell "LOVE"; adhere to vellum. Adhere cover layout to front of book. Attach fibers around outer edge of front cover and thread fibers through cover to tie book together.

Inside pages: Cut handmade-style papers to cover pages. Use computer to generate, or hand-print, captions and quotations on white card stock; cut out and ink edges. Mat photos onto pieces of handmade-style paper; adhere to pages with quotations. Embellish pages with fibers as desired. ■

SOURCES: Book and heart charm from Making Memories; square brads and alphabet stickers from All My Memories.

MATERIALS

- 6-inch-square book with red cover and black pages
- Black-and-white photos
- White card stock
- Handmade-style papers: red, black, white
- White vellum
- Black ink pad
- Decorative fibers
- Silver steel alphabet stickers
- Brads: silver mini, gunmetal large square
- Silver heart eyelet charm
- Eyelet-setting tool
- Double-sided tape
- Craft cement
- Computer with computer fonts (optional)

Memory Album & Box

Designs by SUSAN STRINGFELLOW

Create a unique album for scrapbook pages and other memorabilia, and then create a coordinating box for storage.

BOX

Lightly spray inside of box and lid with dark green paint; add a few light sprays of blue, then a few more of dark green.

Cut green floral printed paper to cover sides of box bottom, folding excess paper over onto bottom; adhere.

Cut green printed paper strips to cover sides of box lid, folding excess paper over onto top of box; adhere. Cut a square of a green printed paper to cover top of box lid; adhere. Cut a 2-inch-wide strip of rings printed paper; adhere over top and down sides of box lid near right edge.

Color top edge of box and bottom edge of lid with gold leafing pen.

Mat photo on pink printed paper; cut out, leaving a narrow border. Rub edges of mat with distress ink; adhere photo to box lid.

Mat detail photo on light green card stock; lightly ink edges of card stock with distress ink. Adhere photo to upper left corner of box lid.

Stamp caption on box lid using alphabet stamps and black ink. Spray box lid with preservative.

Paint chipboard flowers in a variety of shades of pink, yellow and coral. Sand flowers lightly. Pierce flowers and box lid in lower right corner with awl; attach flowers with copper mini brads.

Attach a bow of complementary ribbon to box lid above flowers with decorative copper straight pin.

ACCORDION BOOK

Cut 10 (5-inch) squares of assorted printed papers; adhere to covers and panels of accordion book.

Paint seams between panels with green acrylic paint; rub seams and edges of panels with distress ink. Embellish panels as desired with strips of contrasting printed paper.

Mat photos on light green card stock; cut out, leaving narrow borders. Rub edges of mats with distress ink; adhere panels, attaching some with foam tape for added dimension.

Add captions, names, etc., as desired with alphabet stamps and black ink.

Paint and sand chipboard flowers as for box; attach copper mini brads through centers and bend prongs flat; adhere flowers to panels. Attach copper mini brads and other copper embellishments to twill, fibers and ribbon, and attach to pages as desired.

On last panel, punch three holes close together along edge in upper right corner. Thread ribbons through holes; trim ends at an angle. ■

SOURCES: Printed papers from Basic Grey; chipboard flowers from Making Memories; copper embellishments from Nunn Designs; distress ink from Ranger Industries; gold leafing pen and preservative from Krylon.

MATERIALS

- 6-inch-square papier-mâché box with lid
- 5-inch-square papier-mâché accordion album
- Photos
- Light green card stock
- Printed papers: green, pink, green floral, rings, green/pink circles
- Chipboard flowers
- Copper embellishments: mini brads, decorative straight pins, charms
- Twill tape
- Fibers and ribbons: variegated green/gold/pink/coral
- Spray paints: dark green, blue
- Acrylic craft paint: light green, yellow, shades of pink, coral
- Alphabet stamps
- Black ink pad
- Light tan distress ink
- Gold leafing pen
- Spray-on preservative
- Hole punch
- Paintbrush
- Awl
- Double-sided tape
- Foam tape

Come Walk in My Garden

Designs by LINDA BEESON

Design a personalized garden journal and bookmark to record photos and footnotes of blossoms and blooms.

JOURNAL

Print photo on photo paper to 8 x 10 inches; trim to 3⅝ x 9¾ with focal point positioned along left edge. Trim ⅝-inch-wide strip off right side of photo; reserve.

Trim two pieces of green printed paper to fit front and back covers of composition book to within ½ inch of spine. Cut argyle printed paper to fit over spine and overlap front and back covers by about 1¼ inches. From striped printed paper, cut two ⅜-inch-wide strips to fit over seams between papers on covers and spine. Check fit; adhere paper pieces to each other.

Machine-sew using zigzag stitch down center of ⅜-inch-wide strips with burgundy sewing thread. Adhere cover to composition book with decoupage medium; trim edges and corners as needed.

Sand edges of photo strips; adhere to right side of cover with decoupage medium, leaving ⅛ inch between strips.

Stamp "my garden" on cover as shown with alphabet stamps and black paint; attach alphabet stickers to spell "walk"; transfer letter rub-ons to spell "come" and "in." Stamp swirl off upper right corner with black paint.

Brush cover with two coats decoupage medium.

SOURCES: Printed papers and letter stickers from Scenic Route Paper Co.; foam stamps from Li'l Davis Designs; swirl stamp from PostModern Designs; pigment paint from Plaid; rub-on transfers from Making Memories.

MATERIALS

- Composition book
- Photo on computer disk
- Photo paper
- Printed papers: green print, green/peach/burgundy argyle, peach/burgundy striped
- Stamps: foam alphabet, swirl
- Black pigment paint
- Alphabet stickers
- Alphabet rub-on transfers
- Small craft brush
- Fine sandpaper
- Sewing machine with burgundy thread
- Double-sided tape
- Decoupage medium
- Computer with printer
- Computer fonts

BOOKMARK

Cut bookmark shapes approximately 2½ x 7 inches from argyle and striped printed papers; adhere pieces to each other, wrong sides facing. Round and trim corners as desired.

Use computer to print garden quotation ("A garden is a friend you can visit any time" was used on sample) on words printed paper so that quotation is positioned in upper half of a 1⅛-inch-wide strip; trim paper to that width. Adhere strip near left edge of bookmark.

Machine-sew using zigzag stitch down edges of strip with burgundy sewing thread.

Adhere a strip of tape measure printed paper down bookmark near right edge.

Sand edges of photo; mat on contrasting printed paper and trim, leaving a narrow border. Adhere to bookmark as shown.

Stamp swirl off upper left corner of bookmark with black paint.

Brush bookmark with two coats of decoupage medium.

Hand-stitch button and ribbon to top of bookmark. ■

SOURCES: Printed papers from Scenic Route; swirl stamp from PostModern Designs; pigment paint from Plaid.

MATERIALS

- Photo
- Printed papers: green/peach/burgundy striped, argyle and words; tape measure
- Swirl stamp
- Black pigment paint
- Black button
- Striped ribbon
- Small craft brush
- Fine sandpaper
- Sewing machine with burgundy thread
- Sewing needle and black thread
- Double-sided tape
- Decoupage medium
- Computer with printer

Sweet Baby Brag Book

Design by SANDRA GRAHAM SMITH

This unique book is sure to become a prized possession for proud new grandparents!

MATERIALS

- 5 (3 x 4-inch) photos
- Light blue card stock
- Baby boy–themed printed paper
- White paper
- ⅛-inch eyelets: 5 blue, 3 light blue
- ¼ x 4-inch self-adhesive hook-and-loop fastening strip
- 2¼ x 1¾-inch wire hanger
- Eyelet-setting tool
- Decorative-edge scissors
- ⅛-inch hole punch
- Glue stick
- Adhesive tape

Using pattern provided, cut card from light blue card stock. Score and fold sides toward center along dashed lines.

Using pattern provided, trace around sleeper onto baby boy printed paper; flip pattern and trace around it again. Cut out sleeper pieces; trim leg openings with decorative-edge scissors. Adhere sleeper pieces to folded card sides so that they overlap about 3⁄16 inch down front.

Trim one side of a ½-inch-wide strip of light blue card stock with decorative-edge scissors; adhere down left front edge of sleeper. Punch six ⅛-inch holes, evenly spaced, down card-stock strip. Set three blue and three light blue eyelets in holes, alternating colors.

Adhere short tabs of light blue card stock, trimmed on both sides with decorative-edge scissors, to shoulders of sleeper. Punch a ⅛-inch hole in each; set blue eyelets in holes.

Cut a 3 x 16-inch strip of white paper. Fold strip accordion-style every 4 inches. Adhere last page inside card. Adhere photos to each panel; embellish photos as desired.

Adhere a hook-and-loop strip to facing edges of sleeper, down center.

Tape hanger to back of card so that hook part of hanger is visible. ■

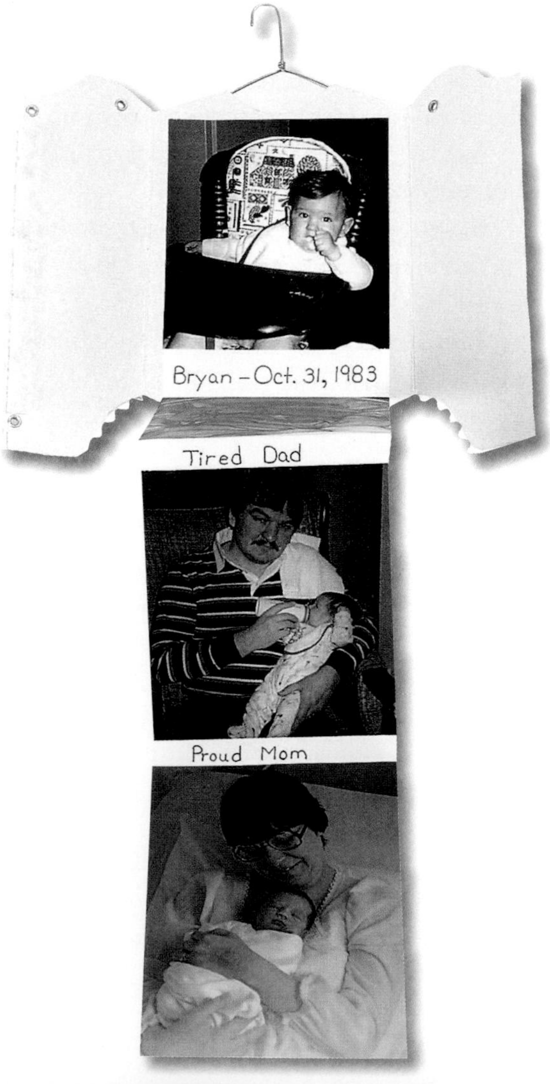

SOURCE: Printed paper from Carolee's Creations.

PATTERNS ON PAGE 157

MATERIALS

- Black multifold photo album with smooth leatherlike cover
- Black-and-white photos on computer disk
- Watercolor canvas sheets
- Rubber stamps: script, numerals
- White ink pad
- Heat gun
- Fabric adhesive
- Computer with printer
- Computer fonts

Boys at the Beach

Design by BARBARA MATTHIESSEN

Nothing is more special than a day at the beach with little boys.

Trim watercolor canvas to fit in printer, trimming off all frayed edges. Type desired captions, titles, dictionary-style definitions, etc., on computer; print out onto watercolor canvas along with photos, feeding canvas sheets into printer one at a time. When ink is dry, cut out individual components and trim.

Stamp a variety of script and numeral motifs horizontally and vertically onto photo album with white ink to create a background design. Heat-set ink with a heat gun.

Adhere trimmed canvas photos, captions, titles and definitions to album cover with fabric adhesive. ■

Beaded Journal

Design by BARBARA MATTHIESSEN

Record your thoughts and dreams in a journal embellished with sparkling beads.

MATERIALS
- Fabric-covered journal or photo album
- Photo on computer disk
- Ink-jet fabric
- Fusible microbeads
- Embellishments as desired: lace trim, pearl bead yardage, decorative buttons, etc.
- Fabric glue
- Iron
- Computer with printer

Print photo onto ink-jet fabric. Trim fabric photo to fit on album cover. Fuse microbeads to photo to cover it completely, following manufacturer's instructions. Adhere beaded photo to cover. Embellish cover as desired. ■

SOURCES: Beads 2 Fuse from The Warm Co.; fabric glue from Beacon.

Count Your Blessings

Count Your Blessings

Design by HEATHER D. WHITE

An altered album filled with photos and special messages will be a treasured gift for years to come.

Opening page: Cut a 6-inch square of solid brown printed paper; ink edges lightly. Cut a 5¾-inch square of ivory polka-dot printed paper; ink edges lightly. Center and adhere to brown square.

Cut a 2 x 6-inch strip of solid pink printed paper; ink edges lightly. Cut a 6-inch strip of ivory/pink printed paper just slightly narrower than solid pink strip; ink edges lightly. Center and adhere ivory/pink printed strip to solid pink strip; adhere both strips over layout near right edge.

Wrap pink ribbon around layout, centering it over the vertical strip; position knot toward bottom of page.

Use computer to generate, or hand-print, "Count Your Many Blessings" on textured light pink card stock to fit within an area 5 x 2 inches. Trim card stock, centering words in a strip 5¾ x 2⅝ inches. Ink edges lightly; adhere card stock across layout as shown.

Use computer to generate, or hand-print, "Name Them One By One" on rose pink card stock to fit within an area 2⅜ x ¼ inches. Trim card stock, centering words in a strip 3 x ½ inches. Ink edges lightly; attach to layout at an angle with silver mini brads.

Lightly ink edges and raised surfaces of white paper flowers; attach to layout with silver mini brads.

Slide layout into first plastic sleeve in album.

Inner pages: Create page layouts as desired, referring to techniques and materials used for inner cover. Add charms, stickers and other embellishments as desired. If desired, trim samples of your child's artwork to size; mat and adhere to a few pages in lieu of photos.

Album cover: Lightly ink edges of a white flower die cut; adhere to square of ivory/blue printed paper to fit in "window." Attach square in the "window" with a large brad at center of die-cut flower. Wrap blue ribbon around cover near spine; knot on front and trim ends at an angle. ■

SOURCES: Album, printed papers, flower die cuts, mini brads and stickers from Making Memories; gunmetal large brads, stencil phrases and charms from All My Memories; ink from Ranger Industries.

MATERIALS

- 6-inch-square album with plastic sleeves
- Photos
- Child's artwork (optional)
- Card stock: textured light pink, rose pink
- Printed papers: solid brown; additional complementary solids and patterns in ivory/brown/pink and brown/blue combinations
- Paper flower die cuts: white, pink, blue
- Metal embellishments: silver mini brads, large gunmetal brads and family-theme stencil phrases, star and silver charms
- Word stickers
- Ribbons and fibers: pinks, blues
- Dark brown ink pad
- ⅛-inch hole punch
- Double-sided tape
- Computer with computer fonts (optional)

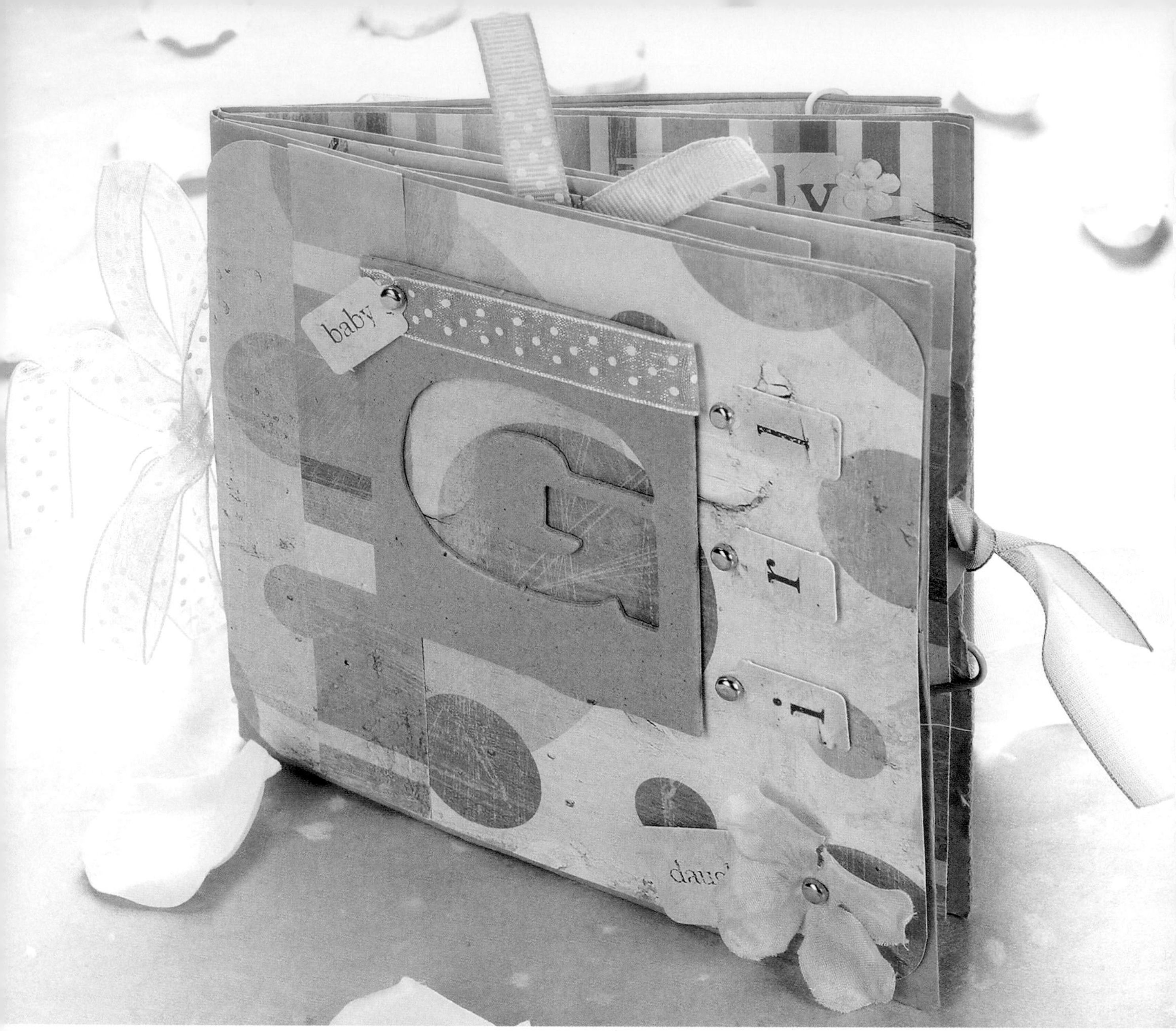

It's a Girl!

Design by SHERRY WRIGHT

More than a typical birth announcement, this keepsake gift doubles as a photo album for family members.

Project note: *Adhere elements using double-sided tape unless instructed otherwise.*

Fold paper bags in half. Punch matching ¼-inch holes on fold, 1 inch from each side. Place one folded bag inside the fold of the other bag, aligning holes. Thread 24 inches ribbon through holes and tie ends in a bow on the outside, forming a paper-bag "book" with four pages—two with open-side edges (top of bags) and two with closed-side edges (bottom fold of bags).

Front cover: Round corners off printed paper cut to cover front of book. Adhere 1-inch-wide strip of complementary printed paper down cover ¾ inch from spine. Ink "G" stencil with pink distress ink; wrap ribbon around top, adhering ends on back. Affix "baby" tag die cut through ribbon in upper left corner of stencil using silver mini brad; adhere stencil to cover layout. Affix mini "i," "r" and "l" tags beside stencil using silver mini brads. Poke silver mini brad through silk flower petals and "daughter" tag die cut; affix in bottom right corner. Tie ribbon bow onto heart charm; adhere to cover layout near bottom left corner using adhesive dot. Adhere cover layout to front of book.

Inside cover: Cut printed paper to cover paper bag; adhere photo with cluster of white flower die cuts in upper right corner. Affix "baby" die-cut tag in upper left corner using matching jumbo brad. Adhere layout inside front cover.

Page 1: Cut printed paper to cover paper bag; adhere library pocket. Write baby's name, birth date and time, weight, length, etc., on library card; staple ribbon at top and slip card into pocket. Adhere "blessing" tag die cut behind slide mount die cut; embellish with mini flower die cut; adhere to front of pocket. Adhere layout to brown paper page.

Page 1 pocket: Use corner rounder punch to trim small photo; adhere photo and pink initial plate to large tag die cut; adhere rub-on transfer verse or saying. Tie ribbon through hole in tag. Tuck tag into open edge of page; hold opening closed with colored paper clip.

Page 2: Cut printed paper to cover paper bag; adhere photo to paper. Affix "miracle" die-cut tag in lower right corner using matching jumbo brad. Adhere layout to brown paper page.

Page 3: Cut printed paper to cover paper bag; adhere photo embellished with tiny flower die cut to bottom left corner. Embellish page with rub-on transfer saying and white flower die cut. Adhere layout to brown paper page; staple ribbon to bottom right corner.

Page 4: Cut printed paper to cover paper bag; adhere photo to paper. Affix "sister" die-cut tag in upper left corner using matching jumbo brad; adhere "sister" word die cut in lower right corner. Adhere layout to brown paper page.

Inside back cover: Cut printed paper to cover paper bag; adhere sister verse to paper. Adhere layout to brown paper page; staple ribbon to bottom right corner.

Back cover: Cut printed paper to cover paper bag; wrap ribbon around upper right corner, adhering ends on back. Apply rub-on transfer onto card stock; trim and adhere to layout; adhere layout to back cover. Hold open edges of bag closed with colored paper clip. ■

SOURCES: Printed papers, library pockets and file folder accessories, including tag die cuts, from Daisy D's Paper Co.; stencil and brads from Making Memories; flower die cuts from Prima; rub-on transfers from Memories Complete; distress ink from Ranger Industries.

MATERIALS

- Photos
- 2 (5½ x 11-inch) brown paper bags
- Complementary card stocks
- Printed papers
- Die cuts: alphabet, word tags, library pocket, tiny white flowers, frame, slide mount
- "G" chipboard stencil
- Baby girl–themed rub-on transfers
- "Sister" verse on card stock
- Pink metal mailbox-style initial plate
- Pale pink distress ink
- Assorted ribbons
- Silver heart charm
- Silk flower petals
- Brads: silver mini, pastel jumbo
- Colored paper clips
- ¼-inch hole punch
- Corner rounder punch
- Stapler with staples
- Double-sided tape
- Adhesive dots

Pocket Album

Design by SHERRY WRIGHT

Pocket–and–library card albums are an ideal way to record memories and milestones in the life of your little one.

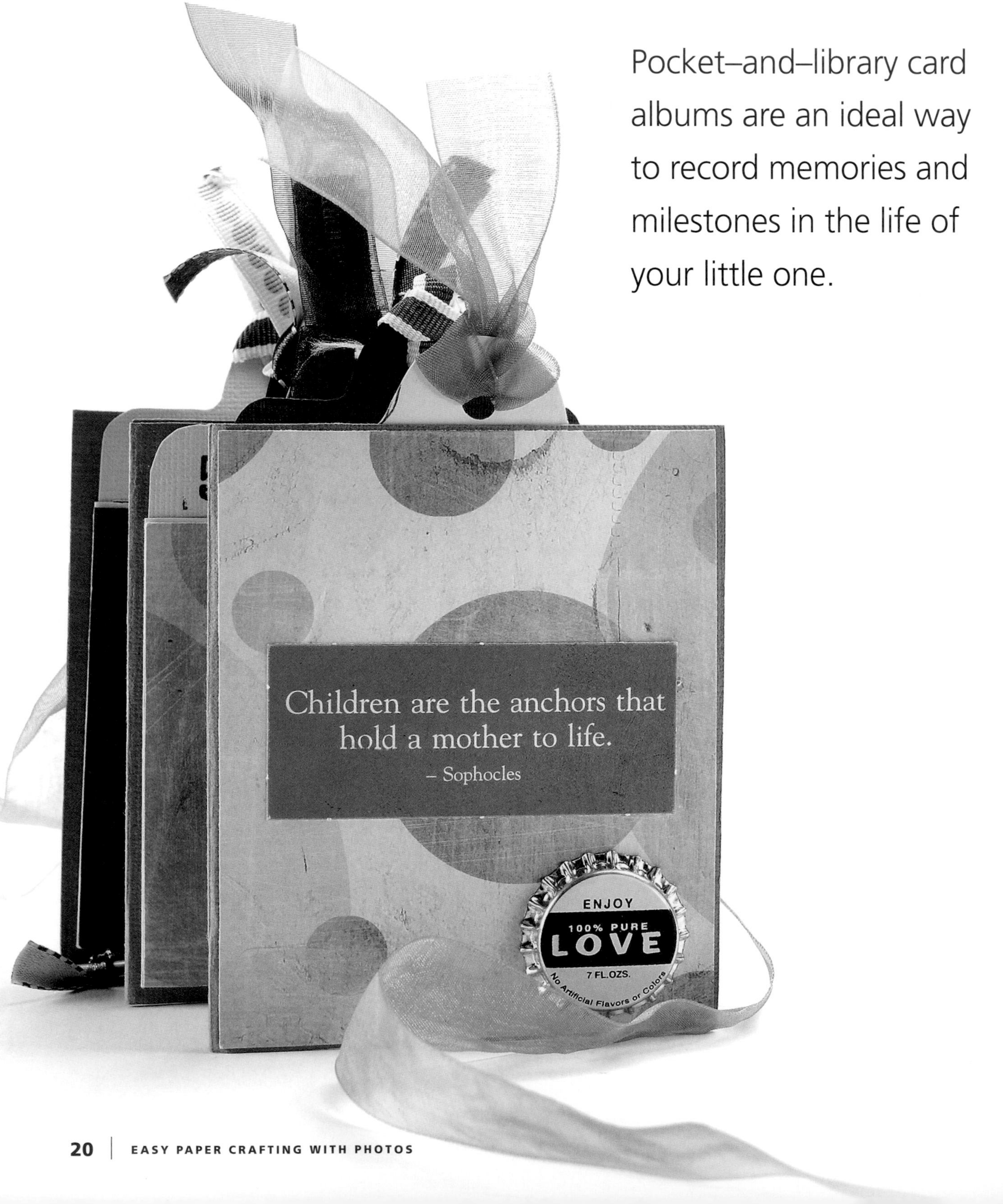

Cut 2 pieces of blue card stock 11½ x 4½ inches; adhere two short edges together, overlapping 3¾ inches to make an 18¾ x 4½-inch strip. Accordion-fold strip every 3¾ inches to make five panels. Cut assorted printed papers to cover library pockets. Adhere pockets to panels in album, on both sides of album, leaving the far right panel on one side and the far left panel on the other side blank. Cover blank panels with printed paper.

Using a tag template, cut eight large tags from red and ivory card stock. ***Option:*** *Draw tag shapes approximately 3¼ x 5 inches on card stock and cut out.* Punch a ¼-inch hole in the end of each tag; thread ribbons and fibers through holes.

Mat photos on card stock and printed paper and adhere to tags and pockets. Add journaling to tags as desired; embellish with large buttons, die-cut tags, stickers, rub-on transfers, stamped images, etc. Add important dates using date stamp. Make labels on label maker—birth time, date, weight, location, etc.—and adhere to pages and tags.

Adhere child-themed sticker and bottle cap to one blank panel on outside of book. To other blank panel, affix hanger hooks at corners; knot ribbons in hangers. Thread sheer ribbon through metal slide; adhere slide to front of album and tie ribbons in a bow to hold album closed. ■

SOURCES: Printed paper, file folder embellishments and metal hangers from Daisy D's Paper Co.; letter stickers from Arctic Frog; rubber stamp from Close To My Heart; bottle caps and chipboard tag from Li'l Davis Designs; ribbon charm and metal plaques from Making Memories; rub-on transfers from Memories Complete.

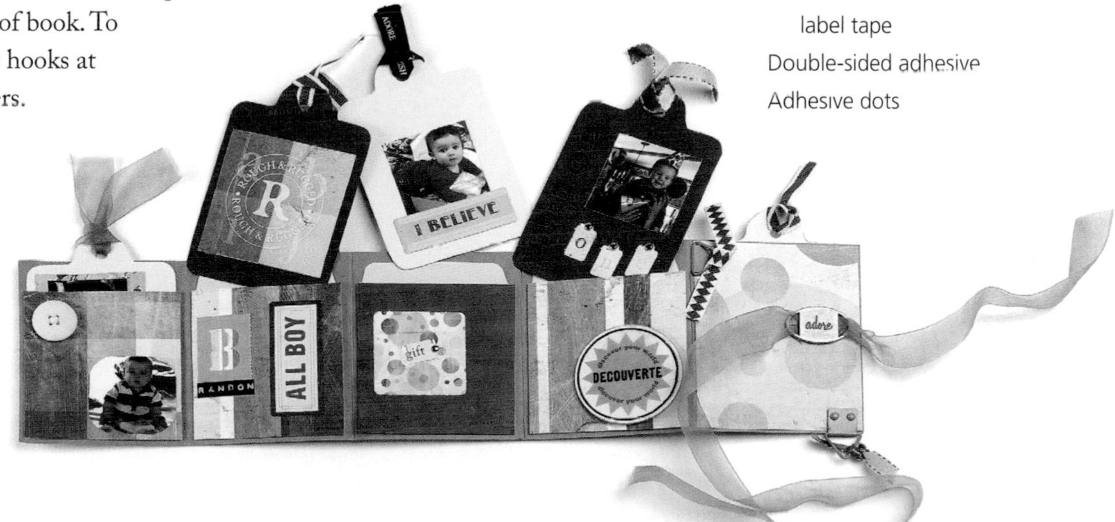

MATERIALS

Small photos
Card stock: blue, red, ivory
Printed paper
Die cuts: 8 library pockets, tags, flowers
Slide mounts
File folder embellishments
Chipboard "Discover"
Child-themed word and alphabet tags, stickers, rub-on transfers
"Celebrate" rubber stamp
Date stamp
Black ink
Bottle caps
Large buttons
Metal hanger hooks
Brads
Assorted ribbons and fibers
¼-inch hole punch
Tag template (optional)
Label maker with label tape
Double-sided adhesive
Adhesive dots

School Days

Design by MARY LYNN MALONEY

Embellish the cover of a basic file folder with paints and photos for an ideal way to store grade-school mementos.

MATERIALS

- Expandable file folder
- School photos
- Card stock: sage green, bright yellow, bright blue
- Light blue printed paper
- Parchment paper
- Ivory printer paper
- Mica pigment watercolor paints: yellow, sea green, blue
- 5 (⅝-inch) self-adhesive round tags with blue metal rims
- ½-inch hole punch
- Circle cutter
- Craft sponge
- Glue stick
- Computer with printer
- Computer fonts (optional)

Lay parchment between flap and front of file folder to protect front. Using a sponge slightly moistened with water, daub flap randomly with yellow paint, keeping sponge wet as you work. Change water; clean sponge, and repeat process with sea green and blue paints. Let dry. Lightly daub bright yellow card stock with blue paint; let dry.

Cut a 20 x 3¼-inch strip from sage green card stock; adhere across front of flap, adhering ends on back. Tear a 2½-inch-wide strip from blue printed paper; center and adhere over sage green strip.

Use circle cutter to cut six 2½-inch circles from sponged yellow card stock, six 2¼-inch circles from bright blue card stock, and five 2-inch circles from school photos. Center and adhere bright blue circles over sponged yellow circles. Center and adhere photographs over five of the layered circles. Adhere circles with photos, evenly spaced, across flap.

Hand-print or use computer to generate child's name to fit on sixth circle; also print grade numbers "K," "1," "2," "3" and "4" to fit within ⅝-inch tags. Print onto ivory printer paper.

Punch grade numbers from ivory paper with ½-inch hole punch; adhere each to metal-rim tag and adhere tag next to appropriate photo. Tear leftover blue printed paper to 3½ x 1 inch; tear strip with child's name in center to 3½ x ½-inch strip. Center and adhere name strip to blue strip; adhere both strips across sixth circle. Trim edges even. Center and adhere circle over edge of flap.

Cut cord closure from expandable file into three equal pieces; knot together. Adhere knot to bottom of name circle on flap. ■

SOURCES: Paints from LuminArte; metal-rim tags from EK Success.

$7.95
for Young Readers
#17
M.D.Spenser
Shivers
Michael
K
1
2
3
4
HB

Be Happy

Design by MARY AYRES

Let this project be a reminder to you to put those worries away and smile for a while!

MATERIALS

- 2 (5½-inch) papier-mâché circle tags
- Black-and-white photo on computer disk
- White canvas paper
- Printed papers: assorted neutrals, solid black
- 1½ x 2¾-inch tea-dyed tag
- White paper sheets
- 12 bottle caps
- Small gold heart charm
- Gold-finish washer*
- Gray fibers
- Alphabet rubber stamps
- Ink pads: black, brown
- Paintbrushes: 1-inch bristle, 3-inch foam
- Hole punches: ¼-inch, ½-inch
- Laminating liquid
- Instant-dry paper glue
- Permanent adhesive
- Adhesive foam squares
- Computer with printer
- Computer fonts (optional)

*Available at home-improvement stores.

To make album front cover, trace around one papier-mâché tag onto solid black paper; cut out. Punch a ½-inch hole in black circle to match hole in tag. Brush back of black circle with bristle brush and permanent adhesive; adhere to papier-mâché tag. Brush front of black circle with foam brush and laminating liquid. Plain papier-mâché tag will serve as back cover.

Print photo onto wrong side of canvas paper. Trim photo into a 4¼-inch circle; center and adhere to album front cover over black paper side with paper glue. Adhere gold-finish washer over hole with permanent adhesive.

Use computer to generate, or hand-print, "happy" words onto assorted neutral printed papers to fit within 1-inch circles. Trace 1-inch circles around words; cut out and adhere to bottle caps with paper glue. Shade edges with brown ink pad.

Adhere bottle caps around edge of album cover with adhesive foam squares. Adhere gold heart charm to one bottle cap with permanent adhesive.

Cut a 5½-inch circle from white paper for each album page; punch a ¼-inch hole in each page to match hole in covers. Stack pages between covers; thread fibers through holes and knot at top of album.

Stamp "Be Happy" on tag with alphabet stamps and black ink. Thread fiber through hole in tag and fiber knot on album; tie ends in a bow. ■

SOURCES: Papier-mâché tags from Walnut Hollow; tag from Rusty Pickle; charm from Nunn Design; alphabet stamps from Plaid/All Night Media; laminating liquid, instant-dry paper glue and gem adhesive from Beacon.

Healthy Challenge

Design by KATHLEEN PANEITZ

Record the journey to a healthier you on the pages of a personalized altered notebook.

MATERIALS

- Composition book
- Photo
- White card stock
- Printed papers: stripes, pink argyle
- Scrap white paper sheet
- Blue alphabet stickers
- "are we having fun yet" die-cut sticker
- Rub-on transfers: "Healthy" and "Journey"
- Pink mailbox-style letter tile
- Brush
- Craft knife
- Decoupage medium
- Computer with computer fonts (optional)

Place a sheet of white scrap paper between cover and first page of the composition book. Brush decoupage medium over cover. Lay stripes printed paper over cover. Turn book over; trim around cover with craft knife. Wipe edges of composition book to remove any decoupage medium; remove white scrap paper.

Mat photo onto white card stock; trim, leaving a narrow border. Adhere photo to cover.

Use a computer to generate, or hand-print, "the challenge to be" and "to being physically fit" on pink argyle printed paper. Trim printed paper around words, leaving room 2 inches below "the challenge to be" for the "H" from "Healthy" rub-on transfer, and 1 inch above "to be physically fit" for placement of mid-section of the "Journey" rub-on transfer. Adhere pink rectangles to cover as shown.

Spell "my" down left side with blue alphabet stickers. Adhere "are we having fun yet" die-cut sticker next to lower pink rectangle, and pink mailbox-style letter tile to upper right corner of photo. Apply "Healthy" and "Journey" rub-on transfers to cover as shown. ■

SOURCES: Printed papers from Junkitz and Rusty Pickle; rub-on transfers from Jeneva & Co. and Making Memories; die-cut sticker and mailbox letter tile from Making Memories; alphabet stickers from Westrim Crafts.

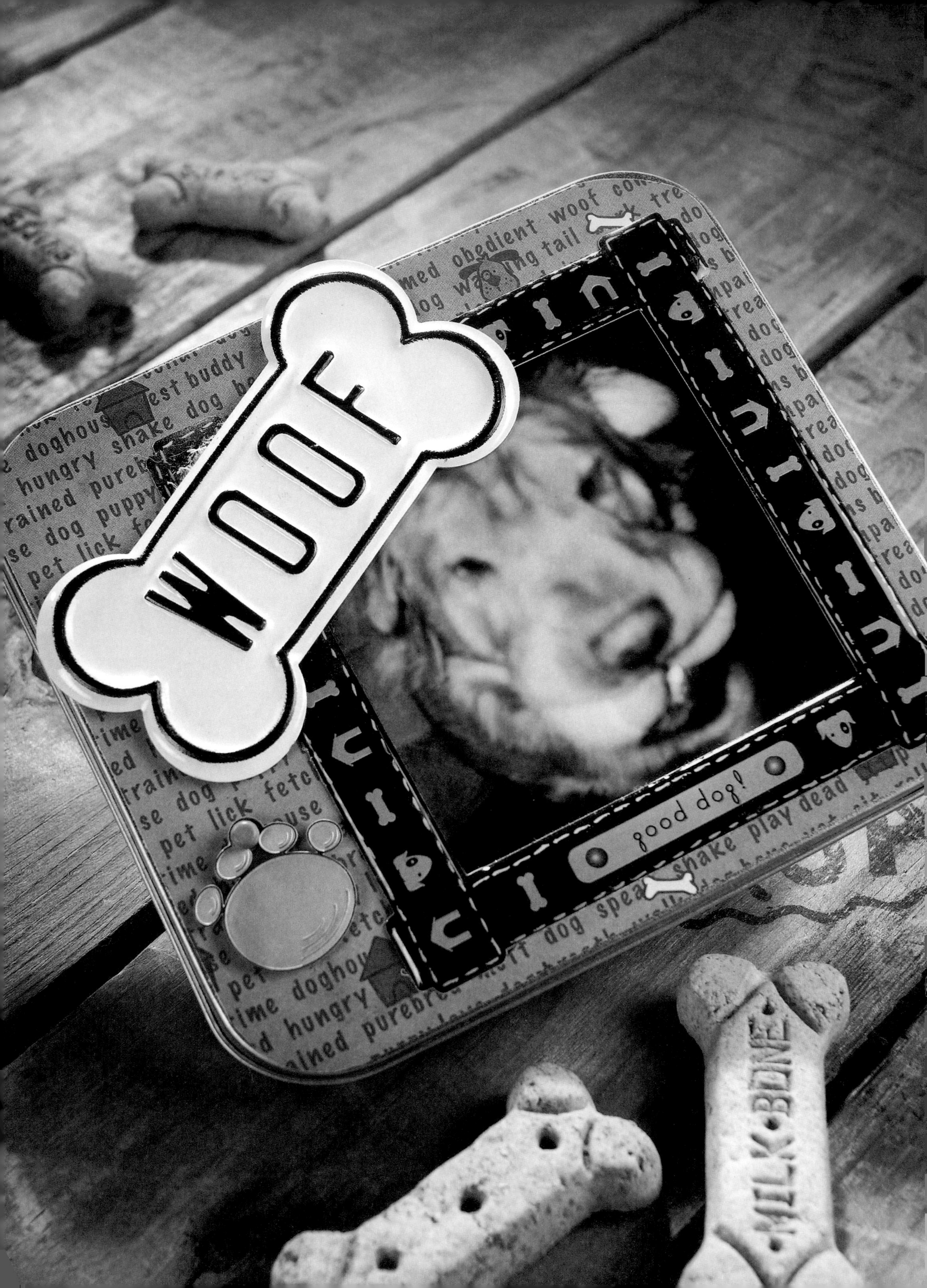
WOOF
good dog!
MILK-BONE

Pet Brag Book

Design by SUSAN HUBER

Pets hold a dear place in our hearts and homes. Create a fun memory book filled with favorite photos of your furry friends.

Lay out six album pages side by side, edges touching. Apply double-sided tape to 10 (1½ x 3½-inch) strips of pet-themed printed paper; lay a piece over each seam to join pages in a continuous strip. After attaching strips to first side, flip pages over and apply remaining strips to seams on other side.

Cut printed card stock and paper to fit on each page between joining strips. Mat photos on printed card stock or paper, or double-mat on cork sheet and card stock, to fit on album pages. Embellish pages as desired with stickers, charms, mini accessories, cork letters and twill tape. Attach charms with mini brads and foam tape; adhere other elements with foam tape and double-sided tape as desired. Adhere first and last pages inside lid and box with double-sided tape. To close box, fold pages accordion style.

Cover: Cut card stock to fit lid. Trim photo to fit behind epoxy frame; adhere photo and frame to card stock. Adhere "WOOF" bone over corner of photo with foam tape. Attach charm to cover layout with foam tape and tan mini brad. Adhere cover layout to lid of tin using double-sided tape. ■

SOURCES: Tin box, printed paper, album pages and charms from Boxer Scrapbook Productions; metal bone, epoxy embellishments, disks and stickers from Sticker Studio; charms from Li'l Davis Designs; cork from LazerLetterz; epoxy stickers from Karen Foster Designs; mini accessories from EK Success; bone brads from Queen & Co.

MATERIALS

- 5½ x 4¾ x ½-inch tin box with lid
- Photos
- Card stock: desired colors and prints
- Pet-themed printed paper
- 6 card-stock album pages
- Stickers: alphabet, epoxy
- Epoxy "good dog!" frame
- "WOOF" metal bone
- Pet charms and mini accessories
- Cork sheet and letters
- Epoxy stickers
- ⅝-inch metal-rimmed disks
- Epoxy domes
- Brads: large, mini, dog bones
- ½-inch-wide red twill tape
- Double-sided tape
- Foam tape

Halloween Hauntings

Designs by SANDRA GRAHAM SMITH

After the party is over, treat the host and hostess to an album filled with fun photos of the festivities.

Cut a 7 x 4¼-inch piece of striped printed paper; fold in half to form 3½ x 4¼-inch cover. Adhere an 8½ x ¾-inch strip of Halloween phrases printed paper around front and back of cover, matching end of strip to edge of cover on front and leaving extra tab protruding on back. Cut a ¾-inch square of orange card stock; trim one edge with decorative-edge scissors and adhere to underside of tab, leaving decorative edge and about ⅜ inch of orange square showing. Set orange pumpkin eyelet in end of tab. Adhere halves of hook-and-loop closure to ends of Halloween phrases strip so that end of strip can be secured on front to close album.

Cut a 2-inch square of purple card stock using decorative-edge scissors; set black bat eyelets along right edge. Adhere square to album cover at an angle. Split slide mount in half; punch three ⅛-inch holes down left side; set orange eyelets in holes. Thread strands of green and purple floss through eyelets. Mount photo behind slide mount. Trim "Halloween" from phrases printed paper; mat onto orange card stock and trim, leaving very narrow border. Adhere tag to right side of slide mount. Adhere slide mount to album cover at an angle, overlapping purple square.

Cut polka-dot printed paper to fit inside of front cover; trim with decorative-edge scissors and adhere. Thread purple and green floss through hole in Halloween word tag; trim. Adhere tag inside album cover.

Cut a strip of white card stock 24 x 4 inches; fold paper accordion-style every 4 inches. Adhere trimmed photos to individual panels, adhering last panel inside back cover of album. Embellish photos as desired with captions, words cut from Halloween phrases printed paper, etc. ■

SOURCE: Printed papers from Creative Imaginations.

MATERIALS

- Photos trimmed slightly smaller than 3 x 4 inches
- Card stock: white, purple, orange
- Printed papers: Halloween-themed phrases, striped, polka dots
- Paper Halloween word tag
- Black slide mount
- Embroidery floss: purple, green
- Eyelets: 3 round orange, 2 black bats, orange pumpkin
- Self-adhesive hook-and-loop dot closure
- Eyelet-setting tool
- Decorative-edge scissors
- ⅛-inch hole punch
- Glue stick

Memories of Winter

Design by ALICE GOLDEN

Fill the folds and pockets of this album with winter memories that are sure to warm your heart.

MATERIALS

- 5 x 6¾-inch white accordion keeper
- Small photos
- Card stock: white, silver
- Printed papers: slate gray, dark blue and light blue crackles; snowflake
- Blue crackle slide mounts
- White 1¾ x 13⁄32-inch tags
- Rubber stamps: winter saying, alphabet
- Inks: silver pigment, dark blue dye, watermark
- Silver embossing powder
- Stickers: blue alphabet, blue paint chips, snowflakes and winter
- Metallic snow definition tag
- Silver epoxy "snow" paper clip
- "Frosty" retro panel
- Nickel photo turns
- Nickel thumbtack brads
- Silver brads: mini, large, snowflake
- Silver eyelets
- White elastic cord
- Silver thread
- Assorted blue fibers and ribbons
- Eyelet-setting tool
- Embossing heat tool
- ¾-inch circle die cutter *or* hole punch
- Instant-dry paper glue
- Craft cement
- Dimensional adhesive dots
- Computer with computer fonts (optional)

Project note: *Adhere paper to paper with instant-dry paper glue; adhere other elements with craft cement.*

Folder: Remove closure that comes with accordion keeper. Ink edge of top flap with watermark ink; coat with silver embossing powder and emboss. Stamp winter saying in corner of flap with watermark ink; sprinkle with silver embossing powder and emboss. Punch or die-cut two ¾-inch circles from silver card stock. Adhere one silver circle to top flap with snowflake brad and other to bottom flap with large silver brad. Tie silver thread around snowflake brad; wrap thread around silver brad to close folder.

Adhere printed papers to cover inner pages. Mat and double-mat photos on printed papers, and embellish and adhere as desired. For example, you may embellish with photo turns attached with nickel brads, or eyelets set in pages with elastic cord threaded through eyelets to accent photo. Frame photo in slide mounts; wrap with silver thread, or split slide mount in half; remove plastic window and mount a photo in each half.

Use mini brads to attach a 3 x 6½-inch panel of printed paper to one page. Use computer or hand-print winter events on white tags and tie ribbons in tag holes. Slip tags behind panel with ribbon ends sticking out.

Make a 3¾ x 5-inch pocket from printed paper and adhere outer edges to page. Make a 2¾ x 5-inch rectangle from white card stock and use computer to generate, or hand-print, winter memory on rectangle. Punch small hole in top and attach metallic tag to rectangle with fibers. Insert rectangle in pocket.

Embellish remaining areas with retro panel, "snow" paper clip, and word panels made from printed papers matted on card stock, attached with dimensional adhesive dots. ■

SOURCES: Accordion keeper from Bazzill; printed papers from Creative Imaginations; instant-dry paper glue from Beacon.

Kenmore, Scotland
quiet, cold
WINTER
warm comforts
brothers
quiet, cold
WINTER
warm comforts

How Does Your Garden Grow?

Design by KATHLEEN PANEITZ

Your passion for gardening will be reflected in the pages of this stunning album.

Project note: *Adhere all cover elements with craft cement.*

Cover: Stamp flower name onto frame with alphabet stamps. Punch holes in corners of frame with eyelet-setting tool; insert mini brads in holes.

Using computer, print photo onto canvas paper. Trim photo; adhere to back of frame.

Use computer to generate, or hand-print, quotation on white vellum to fit within an area 5 x ½ inches. Tear vellum so that the quotation is positioned along top edge of a rectangle approximately 5 x 5½ inches.

Position vellum on album cover with quotation on left edge; top with framed photo, leaving quotation exposed. Attach all layers to cover.

Wrap ribbon around journal cover near spine; tie ends in a bow.

Individual pages: Cut a 6-inch square of card stock in a complementary color. Mount the photo—your own, or one cut from a plant tag, seed packet or gardener's catalog—on the card stock.

Use computer to generate, or hand-print, botanical and varietal names, growing information, personal notes about plants, etc., on card stock, printed paper or tag. Adhere information to page.

Embellish page with stamped images, motifs cut from printed paper, ribbon, decorative brads and mini brads. Slide decorated page layout into plastic insert page.

Assemble album. ■

SOURCES: Album kit and frame from Making Memories; canvas paper from K&Company; vellum from Paper Adventures; alphabet stamps from Harbor Freight; craft cement from Beacon.

MATERIALS

- Embellished album kit with 6-inch-square plastic insert pages
- 4 x 5-inch embossible metal frame
- Photos
- Card stock
- Printed papers
- White vellum
- White canvas paper
- Rubber stamps
- Ink pads
- Embellishments: decorative brads and mini brads, eyelets
- Ribbons: 1½-inch-wide white sheer, complementary colors in assorted widths
- Metal alphabet stamps
- Eyelet-setting tool
- Craft cement
- Double-sided tape
- Computer with printer
- Computer fonts (optional)

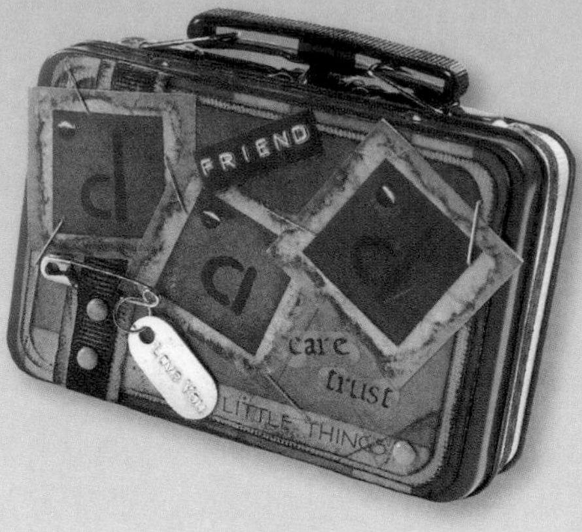

ALTERED ITEMS: BOOKS, CDS, TINS

Altering objects is fun. Add photos and other embellishments to everyday items such as CDs and jars to transform them into works of art!

Coin Holder Photo Album

Design by JULIE RYVER

Loved ones will treasure this unique photo album with spaces for photos of all the family members, no matter how large your family may be.

Cut a 4½ x 5-inch square of striped paper and adhere to lower part of center section of coin holder. Center desired photo on square.

Punch out circles from other photos to fit in coin openings as desired; adhere in openings.

Punch circles from card stock and printed papers to cover other coin openings. Use sponge to ink edges of all circles with black dye ink. Stamp words on punched circles and margins of album. Embellish circles as follows: with heart tile; with tag with stamped word "Cherish" and key with gingham ribbon tied round; with orange card-stock punched star; with silver mini brad in center of black card-stock clock hands, or as desired. Adhere paper and card-stock circles in openings using double-sided adhesive.

Tie black dashed ribbons around creases of coin album. Punch tag from printed paper; embellish with stamped "I love you" and heart brad. Tie tag to one of the crease ribbons near lower edge. On opposite crease ribbon tie lengths of all three ribbons together near upper edge. ■

SOURCES: Coin album from Bazzill; printed paper from Scenic Route Paper Co.; rubber stamps from Technique Tuesday; key from K&Company; heart tile from Making Memories; punches from EK Success.

MATERIALS

- Half-dollar coin holder album
- Small photos
- Card stock: textured green, black, orange and pink
- Printed papers: polka-dots, striped
- Stamps: words, letters
- Black dye ink
- Silver-tone embellishments: mini brad, heart brad, heart tile, metal-rim tag, small key
- Ribbon: black gingham, black dashed, red grosgrain
- Sponge dauber
- Punches: 1½-inch circle, tag, clock hands, star
- Mini adhesive dots
- Double-sided adhesive sheet

Key Ingredients

Design by LAURIE D'AMBROSIO

Pack a pocketful of favorite family recipes inside an altered CD case for a special family reunion gift.

Lid layout: Cut dark green card stock to cover lid; stamp with key stamps and white pigment ink. Heat-set ink.

Adhere a 2 x 5-inch strip of collage printed paper down left side of green card stock; adhere small photo to top block.

Cut a 3 x 1¼-inch piece of rust corrugated card stock. Punch a ⅛-inch hole near bottom edge in center; heat-set a silver doughnut in the hole using the applicator wand and 9mm tip. Attach key through doughnut with jump ring.

Heat-set silver rectangular studs in the shape of desired initial to lower right corner of dark green card stock using the applicator wand and 9mm tip.

Adhere green card-stock layout to lid with glue lines. Attach rust corrugated card stock to center of sheer ribbon with an adhesive dot. Attach center of ribbon to tin lid with three adhesive foam dots; center and adhere rust corrugated card stock over ribbon on lid. When ready to close tin, wrap ribbon around tin and tie in a bow.

Inside lid: Adhere black-and-white checked paper inside lid. Cover photo with shimmer sheet, then mount photo on red card stock; trim, leaving a narrow border.

Pull a row of fringe off each end of a 4-inch piece of beaded trim, leaving an unfringed area on each end of piece. Attach trim across bottom of photo with glue lines, folding the unfringed ends to the back and catching them in the adhesive to secure the fringe. Adhere the photo inside lid with glue lines.

Recipe pocket: Using pattern provided, trace and cut two pockets from white card stock. Trim 1½ inches off the top of one piece; stamp it with key stamps and black ink. Ink edges of both pockets with black ink pad. Heat-set ink.

Hold pockets together, matching bottom edges; punch ⅛-inch holes at dots. Heat-set silver doughnuts in the holes using the applicator wand and 9mm tip. Stitching from left to right, sew pockets together with an overcast stitch and a 24-inch piece of green wire. Repeat, stitching from right to left. Secure wire ends on the back.

Use a computer to generate, or hand-print, desired title or message on white card stock. Tear around edges; ink with green ink pad. Heat-set crystal accents on letters with applicator wand and 2mm tip. Adhere pocket inside tin with glue lines.

Add 3 x 5-inch recipe cards to pocket. ■

SOURCE: Heat-set embellishments and applicator wand from Kandi Corp.

PATTERN ON PAGE 158

MATERIALS

- CD tin
- Photos
- Card stock: dark green, red, white, rust corrugated
- Printed papers: collage, black-and-white checked
- Assorted key rubber stamps
- Ink pads: white pigment, black pigment, emerald green
- Heat-set embellishments: silver rectangular studs, silver doughnuts, 2mm red crystals
- Small key on jump ring
- 1 yard 1-inch-wide sheer white ribbon
- Crystal translucent shimmer sheet
- White beaded fringe trim
- Green 20-gauge wire
- ⅛-inch hole punch
- Heat-setting applicator wand with tips
- Heat gun
- Glue lines
- Adhesive dots
- Adhesive foam dots
- Computer with computer fonts (optional)

Paper & Lace

Design by MARY AYRES

A vintage photo enhanced with subtle chalked color becomes the focal point on this jar wrap.

MATERIALS

- Quart glass canning jar with lid
- High-contrast photo on computer disk
- Ivory card stock
- Printed papers: solid green, streaked, flowers
- Colored chalks
- 2 (¾-inch) brass hinges
- 8 silver mini brads
- 9 (3⁄16-inch) brushed-nickel eyelets
- Assorted pink and green ribbons and fibers
- Lace trim: 1-inch-wide, ¼-inch-wide
- Small gold charm
- Fine sandpaper
- Hole punches: 1⁄16-inch, 3⁄16-inch
- Corner rounder punch
- Sewing machine with ivory thread
- Workable fixative
- Instant-dry paper glue
- Computer with printer
- Computer fonts (optional)

Cut a 3½ x 3¾-inch piece of solid green paper. Print photo on ivory card stock; trim photo to 2½ x 3¼ inches. Color photo with chalks; spray with workable fixative to set colors. Adhere photo to right edge of green rectangle.

Cut a 1 x 3¾-inch strip of flowers paper; adhere to left edge of green rectangle. Trim corners on left side of flowers paper with corner rounder punch. Sand edges of assembled photo rectangle. Machine-stitch around photo on photo near edge with straight stitch and ivory thread; in the same manner, machine-stitch around flowers paper. Adhere ¼-inch-wide lace and tiny fiber bow to dress in photo.

Cut an 8 x 3¾-inch piece of solid green paper. Round corners on right side with corner rounder punch; sand edges. Lay solid green paper rectangles side by side with ⅛-inch space between them and photo on left. Join rectangles with hinges, attaching them ½ inch from top and bottom with silver mini brads. Glue ⅝-inch-wide pink ribbon over seam on back, trimming ribbon even with top and bottom edges of paper.

At each end of joined strip, punch four 3⁄16-inch holes, evenly spaced. Set eyelets in holes. Wrap and adhere hinged photo panel around jar. Beginning in bottom holes, lace ribbon and fibers through eyelets, shoelace style; tie ends in a bow at the top.

Screw lid onto jar. Glue 1-inch-wide lace trim around edge of lid, overlapping ends. Wrap ribbon around lace; tie ends in a bow on right front side.

Tag: Cut a 2½ x 1¼-inch tag shape from solid green paper; mat on ivory card stock and trim around tag, leaving a narrow border. Sand edges. Punch hole in end of tag; set eyelet in hole. Use computer to generate, or hand-print, name or other words on streaked paper; trim around words and adhere streaked paper to tag. Machine-stitch around edges of streaked paper. Thread ribbon through hole in tag; tie tag to ribbon around jar-lid ribbon. ■

SOURCES: Printed papers from KI Memories and Rusty Pickle; workable fixative from Krylon; instant-dry paper glue from Beacon.

Grandma Mary

Lunch Box Treasures

Design by JEANNE WYNHOFF

Embellish a miniature lunch box with children's photos to send off to work with Dad or Grandpa.

NAPA
laugh
treasure
enjoy
learn
loving
life doesn't come with an instruction book, that's why we have fathers.
H. Jackson Brown Jr.

Spray entire lunch box with brown paint; let dry.

Inside lunch box: Cut printed paper to fit inside each lunch-box side. Round off corners with corner rounder and ink with chestnut inkpad as desired.

For first inside side, layer small photos on brown card stock; adhere to paper background using adhesive dots or dimensional adhesive dots to give arrangement depth. Wrap narrow metallic ribbon around edges of photos as desired. Add cork letters, washer word, small heart charm and postmark embellishment. Attach clear word stickers randomly to printed paper. Adhere paper layout in bottom of lunch-box side.

For opposite inside side, embellish paper background with a larger card-stock sticker with stapled-on grosgrain ribbon tags. Adhere metal monogram letter to bottle cap and attach to left of sticker; attach small heart charm to upper right of sticker. Adhere two small card-stock stickers to background paper with mini brad. Adhere paper layout in bottom of lunch-box side.

Outside lunch box: Layer and adhere three printed papers together to fit each side of lunch box.

For first side, wrap two different widths of grosgrain ribbon around long side of layered papers; add a large card-stock sticker and staple over corners that overlap ribbons; stamp "admire" on cork panel; cut out and adhere. Add washer word and "LOVE" label created with label maker. Create "DAD" label on label maker; mount behind a bookplate and attach to paper with mini brads. Adhere assembly to outside side.

For second side, place two lengths of grosgrain ribbon together and secure to layered papers with two mini brads; attach metal "Love You" tag to safety pin and pin between layers of ribbons. Add card-stock alphabet stickers to spell "dad." Add "FRIEND" label made with label maker and clear word stickers as desired. Place a mini brad in one corner and staple randomly across assembly. Adhere assembly to remaining side of lunch box.

Ink edges and surfaces of letters, words and stickers on outside of box as desired.

Ink ribbons as desired; run them through the adhesive applicator and adhere them to outer edges of lunch box and around handle. If desired, mount mini brads in ribbons before adhering them. ■

SOURCES: Printed paper from All My Memories; stickers from All My Memories and Pebbles Inc.; chalk ink from Clearsnap Inc.; spray paint from Krylon; magnetic stamps, washer words and bookplate from Making Memories; cork from LazerLetterz.

MATERIALS

- 4 x 2¾ x 1½-inch mini lunch box
- Small photos
- Brown card stock
- Printed paper in shades of brown
- Dad-themed card-stock stickers
- Chalk ink: chestnut, dark gray
- Brown gloss-finish spray paint
- Bottle caps
- Postmark embellishment
- Mini brads
- Metal monogram letter
- Tiny safety pin, metal "Love You" tag with jump ring and small heart charms
- Washer words and clear word stickers
- Metal bookplate
- Cork panel and letters
- Ribbons: assorted grosgrain and narrow metallic
- Corner rounder punch
- Label maker with label tape
- Adhesive dots and dimensional adhesive dots
- Adhesive applicator

Zoo Trip

Design by LINDA BEESON

Create a personalized DVD case to safely store digital photos from all your favorite family outings.

MATERIALS

- CD/DVD box
- Small photos
- Green textured card stock
- Printed papers: green with letters and numbers, earth-tones circle print
- Alphabet stamps
- Black pigment paint
- Brown fluid chalk ink pad
- Date rub-on transfers
- Double-sided tape
- Foam tape

Trim green card stock to fit around DVD box; adhere. Embellish cover with strips and panels of printed paper as desired, inking edges with brown ink pad; adhere to cover with double-sided tape.

Stamp "Zoo trip" on left side of cover with alphabet stamps and black paint.

Cut a rectangle from green card stock to fit on right side of cover; round off corners. Trim photos to fit on green card-stock rectangle; round off corners. Ink edges of rectangle and photos with brown fluid ink. Adhere photos to rectangle with double-sided tape; adhere rectangle to cover with foam tape.

Transfer date rub-ons onto cover. ■

SOURCES: Printed papers from Basic Grey and Scenic Route; alphabet stamps from Technique Tuesday and Li'l Davis Designs; pigment paint from Plaid; chalk ink pad from Clearsnap Inc.; rub-on transfers from Autumn Leaves.

Fierce Jungle Cat

Design by SUSAN STRINGFELLOW

If your kitty thinks he's the fiercest cat in the jungle (even if the jungle is only your living room), this is the ideal project for you!

MATERIALS

- CD
- Background photo printed in a lighter tone on lightweight matte photo paper
- Featured photo printed on satin photo paper
- Black card stock
- Animal print printed paper
- Alphabet rubber stamps
- Black powdered pigment
- Green card-stock circular paper clip
- Iron-on metallic gold fine cord
- 5⁄16-inch-wide bronze ribbon
- Gold lion charm
- Green silk leaf
- Antiqued mini safety pin
- Bronze/gold/green beaded trim
- Fine sandpaper
- Magnet strips
- Iron
- Permanent adhesive

Sand surfaces of CD so that paper will adhere. Trace around CD onto animal print paper; cut out and adhere paper to front of CD. Ink edges of CD using black pigment. Fuse strips of iron-on gold cord across CD to accent paper's pattern.

Sand edges of lighter background photo; adhere to upper right quadrant of CD. Mat featured photo on black card stock; trim, leaving a narrow border. Adhere photo to left side of CD. Stamp "fierce jungle cat" onto card-stock paper clip; ink edges using black pigment. Attach paper clip over upper left edge of CD.

Tie ribbon in small bow; attach bow and lion charm to green silk leaf using mini safety pin. Adhere leaf to bottom right quadrant of CD. Adhere beaded trim across back bottom edge of CD. Adhere magnet strips to back of CD. ■

SOURCES: Printed paper from The Paper Co.; rubber stamps from EK Success; powdered pigment from Jacquard Products; card-stock paper clip from Deluxe Designs; iron-on cord from Kreinik; beaded trim from Altered Pages.

Girlfriends

Design by TAMI MAYBERRY

Turn an ordinary clipboard into artwork that celebrates the very special relationship between girlfriends!

MATERIALS

- Clipboard
- Photos
- Ivory card stock
- Printed papers: burlap, tan, bittersweet/tan floral
- "Girlfriends" picture
- Tan/gold adhesive mesh
- Brown distress ink
- Metal embellishments: "friends" ribbon slide, "treasures" tiny tag, "friendship" tile
- Ribbons: 3/16-inch-wide brown, gold and burgundy gingham, 5/8-inch-wide bittersweet satin
- Small craft brush
- Decoupage medium
- Craft cement
- Computer with color printer (optional)
- Computer fonts (optional)

Project notes: *For sample project, photos were printed in a sepia tone; "Girlfriends" hens picture was peeled from a cork-backed coaster. Adhere ribbons, photos and other paper elements with a foam brush and decoupage medium. Adhere metal embellishments with craft cement.*

Cut strips of burlap printed paper to cover about 2½ inches of bottom edge of clipboard and upper corners adjacent to clip; adhere, clipping edges of paper around curves and bending them over the edge, onto the back.

Cut a second printed paper to cover remainder of clipboard; adhere, bending edges over onto the back.

Embellish surface of clipboard with ribbons and adhesive mesh. Attach "friends" metal slide to ribbon as shown, layering gingham ribbon over satin ribbon.

Use computer to generate, or hand-print, girlfriends quotation in burgundy onto ivory card stock to fit within an area 5½ x 1¼ inches; trim card stock, centering quotation in an 8½ x 1¾-inch strip. Ink card stock lightly with distress ink; adhere across bottom of clipboard.

Mount photos and "Girlfriends" hens picture onto ivory card stock that has been inked lightly with distress ink; trim, leaving a narrow border. Adhere photos and pictures to clipboard.

Adhere "treasures" charm, "friendship" tile and other embellishments as desired. Knot lengths of gingham ribbon around metal clip. ■

Girlfriends
friends
Laugh and the world laughs with you;
Cry and you cry with your girlfriends.
Treasures

Girl Talk

Design by SANDRA GRAHAM SMITH

Do you know someone who is always chitchatting with the girls? This is the perfect project for her!

MATERIALS

- CD
- Photo of girl on phone
- Card stock: purple, bright yellow
- Printed paper: girl-talk-themed, striped
- Gossip rubber stamp
- Black ink pad
- Adhesive-backed magnets
- Fine sandpaper
- Double-sided adhesive sheet

Sand surfaces of CD so that paper will adhere. Trace around CD onto striped paper; cut out and adhere paper to front of CD.

Mat photo onto purple card stock; cut out, leaving a narrow purple border. Adhere photo to CD.

Cut out sayings and words; adhere to CD.

Ink gossip stamp; stamp onto bright yellow card stock. Trim card stock and adhere to CD.

Adhere magnets to back of CD. ■

SOURCES: Printed papers from Doodlebug Design Inc. and KI Memories; rubber stamp from The Rubbernecker Stamp Co.

Sisters

Design by SANDRA GRAHAM SMITH

Celebrate the special bond between sisters with a personalized altered CD.

MATERIALS

- CD
- Vintage photo
- Card stock: bright pink, black
- Pink roses printed paper
- 1¼-inch Victorian-print tag
- Scraps of old lace trim
- Pink and black embroidery floss
- Gold rose charm
- Adhesive-backed magnets
- Fine sandpaper
- Punches: lace border, ⅛-inch hole
- Double-sided adhesive sheet
- Tape
- Glue stick
- Tacky glue
- Computer with computer fonts (optional)

Sand surfaces of CD so that paper will adhere. Trace around CD onto rose printed paper; cut out and adhere paper to front of CD.

Attach lace trim around edge of CD with tacky glue, leaving area at bottom open for photo.

Punch lace strips from pink card stock with lace border punch; tape to back of photo to frame it. Adhere photo to CD.

Use computer to generate, or hand-print, sister-themed sayings, verses and captions on roses printed paper. Trim around words; mat on black card stock and trim, leaving narrow black borders. Adhere words to CD.

Mat tag on pink card stock and trim, leaving narrow border. Punch ⅛-inch hole in end of tag. Thread pink and black floss through hole; knot and trim ends.

Adhere tag at top of CD; adhere rose charm to CD.

Adhere magnets to back of CD. ■

SOURCE: Tag from K&Company; lace punch from Fiskars.

Earth laughs in flowers
bloom

Patchwork Photo Purse

Design by MARY AYRES

Transform a simple straw handbag into a stylish fashion accessory with the addition of a floral patchwork design.

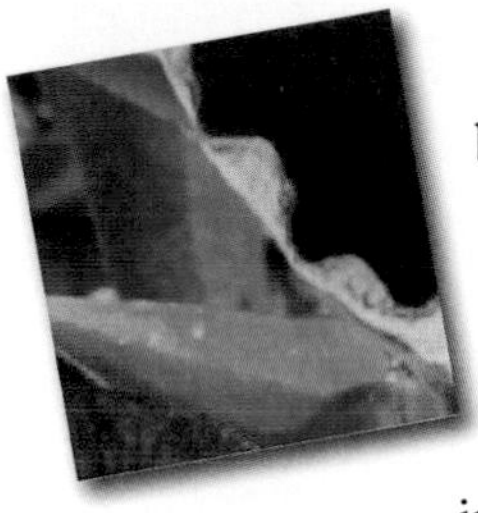

Cut a 6-inch square from medium brown card stock; ink edges with brown ink and dry sponge. Print flower photo to 5 x 7 inches on no-sheen photo paper. Trim photo, centered, into a 4½-inch square; cut square into three 1½-inch-wide strips and cut strips into three 1½-inch squares each. Adhere squares to medium brown card stock, leaving ¼ inch between squares and omitting the center square. Adhere iron-on vinyl to card stock over photos, following manufacturer's instructions; trim vinyl edges even with card stock.

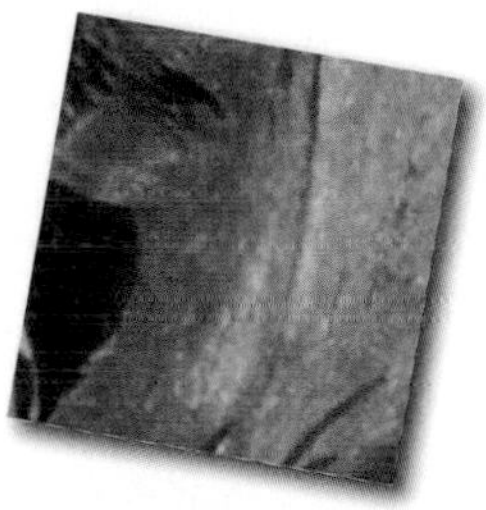

Machine-stitch around photo squares with zigzag stitch and black thread. Use computer to generate, or hand-print, "bloom" on light green card stock to fit in bookplate; trim card stock to fit and adhere to bookplate. Attach bookplate to center of photo panel with black mini brads. With 1/16-inch circle punch, punch holes around medium brown card stock ¼ inch from edge. Adhere medium brown card stock to center of purse, avoiding holes. Stitching through punched holes, whipstitch card stock to purse with tapestry needle and purple pearl cotton; knot ends together inside bag.

Tag: Use computer to generate, or hand-print, "Earth laughs in flowers" on white card stock; trim, leaving room for eyelet on left end. Ink edges with purple ink and dry sponge. Machine-stitch over edges of tag with zigzag stitch and black thread. Punch 3/16-inch hole in end of tag; set eyelet in hole. Tie ribbon in a bow around handle. Tie tag to center of bow with purple pearl cotton. ■

SOURCES: Iron-on vinyl from Therm O Web; instant-dry paper glue from Beacon.

MATERIALS

- Brown straw purse with approximately 8½-inch-square front
- High-contrast, close-up photo of flower on computer disk
- No-sheen photo paper *or* presentation paper
- Card stock: medium brown, light green, white
- Iron-on vinyl
- Ink pads: brown, purple
- Brushed-silver oval bookplate
- Black mini brads
- 3/16-inch brushed-nickel eyelet
- Purple pearl cotton *or* needlecraft thread
- Sheer light green polka-dot ribbon
- Dry sponge
- Iron
- Hole punches: 1/16-inch, 3/16-inch
- Eyelet-setting tool
- Sewing machine with black thread
- Tapestry needle
- Instant-dry paper glue
- Computer with printer
- Computer fonts (optional)

Cherish
SWEET
HANDSOME
LOVE

Magnetic Photo Easel

Design by JEANNE WYNHOFF

A metal easel becomes the ideal surface to display photos. Create unique magnets to keep them in place!

Spray entire easel with semi-flat black paint; let dry.

Cut printed paper to cover front of easel; round top corners using corner rounder punch. Adhere printed paper to easel with double-sided tape. Randomly stamp paper with patterns using foam stamps and black ink pad. Ink edges of paper covering easel with indigo ink pad.

Mat photos on printed paper. Rough up edges with edge scraper and ink edges lightly with the indigo ink pad. Paint game-board stars metallic silver with foam brush; when dry, ink edges with indigo ink pad. Attach black mini brads through centers of stars. Snap magnetic circle in half; attach one to back of each larger star using adhesive dots. Print desired words on label maker; cut apart and attach to easel.

Arrange photos on easel; hold in place with magnet-backed stars. ***Option:*** *For permanent placement, adhere photos with adhesive dots, double-sided adhesive or foam tape; adhere game-board stars in the same manner, stacking several thicknesses of foam tape for some pieces to give the arrangement added dimension.*

Lightly ink a strip of twill tape with black and sepia ink pads; thread through hole in luggage tag. Ink luggage tag completely with black ink pad. Cut a larger tag shape from printed paper; ink edges of this tag and punch-out initial with indigo ink pad. Layer larger printed paper tag, luggage tag and initial on easel.

Ink fibers; wrap across front of easel as desired. Run a thin strip of leather through adhesive applicator; thread on alphabet charms and adhere across bottom of easel.

Using a combination of the label maker, alphabet stamps and stickers, fill in spaces with names and endearing words—"handsome," "treasure," "love," "sweet," etc. Punch circles from printed paper; attach page pebbles over top and adhere to easel. Adhere heart brads. ■

SOURCES: Printed papers from Basic Grey; foam stamps, game-board stars and page pebbles from Making Memories; luggage tag from LazerLetterz.

MATERIALS

- Metal easel
- Photos
- Printed paper
- Card-stock stickers
- Punch-out alphabet letters
- Luggage tag
- Foam stamps
- Ink pads: black, sepia, indigo
- Paint: semi-flat black spray paint, silver metallic craft paint
- Brads: silver hearts, black mini
- Epoxy stickers: words, page pebbles
- Game-board stars
- Ribbon slide alphabet charms
- Thin leather strip
- Fibers and twill tape
- Magnetic circles
- Edge scraper
- Corner rounder punch
- Label maker with label tape
- Foam brush
- Adhesive foam dots
- Adhesive dots and dimensional adhesive dots
- Adhesive cartridge with applicator
- Double-sided tape

American Pride

Design by SUSAN STRINGFELLOW

Display your love of our great country with a piece of altered art that you'll be proud to display all year long.

MATERIALS

- CD
- Photo printed on satin photo paper
- Navy card stock
- Patriotic-themed printed paper
- Alphabet rubber stamps
- Black solvent-based ink
- Photo inks: linen, antique
- ⅝-inch-wide burgundy grosgrain ribbon
- "Freedom" eyelet charm
- Silver star charm
- Red mini brad
- Navy blue craft wire
- Assorted glass beads: red, white, blue, gold
- Fine sandpaper
- Round-nose pliers
- Craft cement

Sand surface of CD so that paper will adhere. Trace around CD onto patriotic printed paper; cut out and adhere paper to front of CD. Ink edges of CD using antique photo ink.

Trim photo, leaving narrow white border. ***Option:*** *Mount photo on white card stock; trim, leaving narrow border.* Ink edges of photo using linen photo ink. Mount matted photo on navy card stock; trim, leaving a narrow border. Adhere photo over left two-thirds of CD. Cut words from patriotic printed paper; adhere diagonally across bottom of photo. Attach red mini brad through edge of photo mat just above lower left corner.

Adhere "freedom" eyelet charm to navy card stock; trim around charm, leaving narrow border. Adhere charm in lower right quadrant of CD, over edge. Adhere star charm over upper right edge of photo.

Curl end of a 6-inch piece of wire in a flat spiral. Thread beads randomly onto wire for 3½ inches; curl remaining wire in a flat spiral. Bend slight wave into beaded wire; adhere across lower portion of CD.

Stamp "4th of July" along right edge of CD using alphabet stamps and solvent-based ink. Fold 18-inch length of burgundy ribbon into a loop; adhere across back of CD. ■

SOURCES: Rubber stamps from Rubber Stamp Ave.; solvent-based ink from Tsukineko; photo inks from Ranger Industries; charms from Making Memories.

You Are Loved

Design by GWEN TAYLOR

Decoupaged photos and papers dress up this wooden surface to create a work of art!

MATERIALS

- Cutting board
- Photos
- Peach card stock
- Printed papers: brown/peach/turquoise geometrics and swirls
- Reddish-brown acrylic paint
- Alphabet stamps
- Ink pads: brown, black
- Alphabet rub-on transfers
- "U for understanding" stencil tag
- Alphabet stickers
- Small heart charm with jump ring
- Metal alphabet disks to spell "Loved"
- Small mosaic tiles: shades of brown, turquoise
- Complementary turquoise/brown/peach ribbons
- Fine sandpaper
- Paintbrush
- Double-sided tape
- Craft cement

Clean cutting board; sand until smooth. Paint with acrylic paint.

Cut shapes from printed papers for background; round corners and ink edges with ink pad. Adhere shapes to cutting board as desired with double-sided tape.

Round corners of photos. Mat photos on card stock and trim, leaving borders and areas for lettering as desired. Ink edges of mats with ink pad. Add captions, names, etc., with stamps and ink, and/or rub-on transfers. Adhere mounted photos to cutting board using double-sided tape.

Attach heart charm to ribbon with jump ring; tie ribbon around cutting board through handle.

Adhere "U" stencil tag to right side of printed paper; trim edges even. Tie ribbon through hole in tag; adhere tag to cutting board in upper left corner with double-sided tape. Adhere alphabet stickers to spell "are" next to handle on right side. Adhere metal alphabet disks to spell "Loved" down right side of cutting board with craft cement.

Adhere additional ribbon accents as desired with double-sided tape. Adhere mosaic tiles with craft cement. ■

SOURCES: Printed papers from Grassroots; alphabet stamps from Leave Memories; ink pads from Ranger Industries; rub-on transfers and metal alphabet disks from Making Memories; stencil from Autumn Leaves; alphabet stickers from All My Memories; mosaic tiles from Magic Scraps; craft cement from JudiKins.

Heirlooms

Design by SHERRY WRIGHT

A tiny piece of altered art becomes a place of safekeeping for small family treasures.

MATERIALS

- Mint tin
- Small photos
- Cream card stock
- 2¾ x 3½-inch tag
- Postal-themed stickers
- Small metal photo frame
- Metal stencil tile with desired initial
- Spiral metal clip
- Family-themed metal word die cuts and quotation tile
- Distress ink
- Black solvent ink
- Cream craft paint
- Ribbons
- Torn fabric strip
- Fine sandpaper
- Paintbrush
- Double-sided adhesive
- Adhesive dots

Project note: *Adhere elements using double-sided tape unless instructed otherwise.*

Sand tin to remove markings. Paint lid cream. Let dry.

Adhere ribbon across lower front of lid. Thread additional ribbon through hole in tag; adhere tag to right side of lid. Adhere postal-themed stickers, spiral metal clip, and "family" metal die cut. Ink metal initial tile with black solvent ink; adhere over tag. Mount photo in frame; adhere to left side of lid.

Adhere a collage of postal-themed stickers to inside of lid. Top with metal family-themed quotation tile.

Mini photo album: Cut a 3 x 12-inch strip of cream card stock; ink or paint as desired. Fold card-stock strip accordion-style every 2 inches. Tuck small photos between folds; tie shut with torn fabric strip. Tuck "cherish" metal die-cut word under fabric strip. Store mini photo album in tin. ■

SOURCES: Stickers from K&Company; frame from Pebbles Inc.; stencil tile from Scrapworks; metal clip, metal die cuts and quotation tile from Making Memories.

Altered Time

Design by SHERRY WRIGHT

Dad will treasure this altered clock—a special piece of decor for his office or shop.

MATERIALS

- 8-inch-diameter round clock
- Photo
- Bottle caps printed paper
- Plain paper
- Stickers: license plate-style large and small numbers, stars, small alphabet, road sign
- "One of a kind" rub-on transfer
- 2 bottle caps
- Mailbox-style initial
- Compass
- Rubber mallet
- Double-sided adhesive
- Adhesive dots

Take clock apart; remove hands. Measure circumference of clock face with compass; draw a paper pattern of the entire clock face on plain paper. Transfer the measurements to the bottle cap printed paper; cut out. Adhere printed paper to clock face.

Use compass to make a 2½-inch pattern from plain paper; trace circle on photo and cut out. Adhere photo to clock face in upper left-hand corner. Adhere large number stickers at 12, 3, 6 and 9 o'clock positions. Adhere star stickers between the number stickers. Adhere small number stickers to road-sign sticker to indicate the year—06, etc. Adhere mailbox initial to clock face.

Flatten bottle caps with rubber mallet. Adhere small letter stickers "a" and "d" to one bottle cap to spell "Dad"; rub on "One of a kind" transfer onto the other. Adhere bottle caps to clock face.

Reassemble clock. ■

SOURCES: Printed paper from Rusty Pickle; license plate stickers from Sticker Studio; rub-on transfer from Li'l Davis Designs; mailbox initial from Making Memories.

HOME DECOR

It's easy to keep favorite photos on display at all times. Here are more than a dozen ways to show off your photos, and not one involves a frame!

Mini Page Coasters

Design by STACEY STAMITOLES

Scrapbook pages reduced to fit the surface of tumbled tiles become a set of handy drink coasters.

Wipe the tiles with a damp cloth to remove dust. ***Option:*** *Color edges of tiles with ink, paints or chalks.*

Coat the back of a reduced scrapbook page layout with decoupage medium. Press the layout onto a tile; smooth out bubbles with your fingers. Brush the top of the tile with decoupage medium. Let dry, then brush with a second coat.

Brush all surfaces of coaster with outdoor sealer. ***Option:*** *Adhere protective cork or felt to bottom of coasters.* ■

MATERIALS

- 4-inch-square tumbled tiles
- Reduced-size photocopies of scrapbook page layouts, 3–3½ inches square
- Inks, paints *or* chalks (optional)
- Outdoor sealer
- Protective cork *or* felt backing (optional)
- Damp cloth
- Foam brush
- Decoupage medium

blooming
memories

"Sara" Tin

Design by MARY AYRES

Transform a simple metal tin into a stylish keepsake container for your favorite teenager!

Butterfly panel: Cut a 5 x 3½-inch rectangle from mint green card stock; round off corners with corner punch. Using pattern provided (page 160), cut butterfly *wings only* from pink tiny alphabet printed paper. Center and adhere wings to mint green rectangle.

Machine-stitch around wings close to edge with straight stitch and white thread. Machine-stitch around edges of rectangle with zigzag stitch and white thread.

Cut butterfly *body only* from striped printed paper; glue to butterfly.

Punch a 1-inch circle around each photo; trim with decorative-edge scissors. Glue photos to upper wings. Punch two 1-inch circles from striped printed paper; trim with decorative-edge scissors and glue to bottom wings.

Punch two ½-inch circles from striped printed paper; glue to centers of 1-inch circles on wings. Punch 1⁄16-inch hole in the center of each ½-inch circle; set pink mini brads in holes. Punch three 1⁄16-inch holes across wings on each side of body; set green and yellow mini brads in holes.

Punch two ⅛-inch holes in green card stock near butterfly's head; set silver eyelets in holes. Thread wire through eyelets and curl wire ends to form antennae.

Punch a 3⁄16-inch hole in each corner of the green rectangle; set eyelets in holes. Thread green ribbon through top eyelets and pink ribbon through bottom eyelets. Wrap ribbons around tin, centering green rectangle on one side, and tie the ribbon ends in bows at opposite corners.

Label: Use computer to generate, or hand-print, "blooming memories" on light yellow card stock to fit in bookplate on side of tin. Cut out words; slide label into bookplate.

Lid: Cut a 5½-inch square from green alphabet printed paper; round off corners with corner punch. Cut a 5½ x 2-inch strip from pink card stock; center and adhere strip to square.

Machine-stitch around edge of square, over ends of pink strip, using a zigzag stitch and white thread. Machine-stitch along long edges of pink strip, close to edge, using a straight stitch and white thread.

Arrange die-cut letters on pink strip; punch a ⅛-inch hole in top of each letter and affix letters with assorted mini brads. Affix gold flower to lid layout with a pink mini brad.

Center and adhere layout to lid. ■

SOURCES: Printed papers, die-cut letters and ribbons from KI Memories; gold flower from Nunn Design; instant-dry paper glue from Beacon.

PATTERN ON PAGE 160

MATERIALS

- 6-inch-square tin with bookplate and lid
- 2 (1-inch) mirror-image black-and-white photos
- Card stock: mint green, light yellow, pink
- Printed papers: pink tiny alphabet, green alphabet, assorted striped
- 1½-inch die-cut alphabet letters in assorted prints
- 1⅝-inch gold metal flower
- Mini brads: yellow, light green, pink
- Silver eyelets: 2 (⅛-inch), 4 (3⁄16-inch)
- ¼- to ⅜-inch-wide printed ribbons: pink, light green
- 4 inches 24-gauge light green wire
- Corner rounder punch
- 1-inch circle punch
- Hole punches: 1⁄16-inch, ⅛-inch, 3⁄16-inch, ½-inch
- Decorative-edge scissors
- Eyelet-setting tool
- Sewing machine with white thread
- Instant-dry paper glue
- Computer with computer fonts (optional)

Blooming Treasure Box

Design by SANDRA GRAHAM SMITH

Whether it's a gift for you or for a special friend, this photo-covered keepsake box will be treasured for years to come!

MATERIALS
- Wooden cigar box
- 4 (1-inch) wooden ball knobs
- Color copies of flower photos
- Stickers: "growing"; ladybug; dimensional trowel, garden fork and butterfly
- Craft paints: metallic gold, white
- Foam brush
- Sharp craft knife
- Laminating liquid
- Craft cement

Paint ball knobs metallic gold. Paint cigar box white. Let dry.

Arrange photos on lid and over edges onto sides of cigar box, leaving narrow white borders between photos. Trim photos as needed to accommodate hardware.

Working on one area at a time, coat the cigar box with laminating liquid. Adhere photos to box in wet laminating liquid, smoothing wrinkles with your fingers. Brush additional laminating liquid over the photos. Continue until box and lid are covered with photos and all photos have been coated with laminating liquid.

Adhere painted ball knobs to bottom of box with craft cement for box feet. Let dry.

Center and adhere "growing" sticker to lid. Arrange and adhere remaining stickers to lid as desired.

Carefully slice through photos along seam between lid and box with a sharp craft knife. ■

SOURCES: Stickers from K&Company; laminating liquid from Duncan; craft cement from Eclectic Products.

Cockatoo Switch Plate

Design by SUSAN STRINGFELLOW

A switch plate covered with a photo to coordinate with your decor is the finishing touch to any room.

Cut printed paper ½ inch larger than switch plate. Brush back of paper with decoupage medium; center and adhere paper to switch-plate cover. Smooth out any wrinkles with your fingers. Notch and clip edges of paper, mitering corners and folding edges over onto back. Trim openings for screws and light switch with craft knife.

Trim photo to fit on switch-plate cover. Brush back of photo with decoupage medium; adhere photo to switch-plate cover. Trim openings for screws and light switch with craft knife. ***Option:*** *Ink cut edges of photo with ink pad.*

Spray switch-plate cover with preservative.

Adhere fibers across bottom of switch-plate cover with glue. Adhere remaining embellishments as desired, fastening mini brad through the center of the silk flower. ■

SOURCES: Printed paper from Basic Grey; bamboo clip from 7gypsies; preservative spray from Krylon.

MATERIALS

- Single metal switch-plate cover
- Photo printed on matte-finish photo paper
- Complementary printed paper
- Ink pad (optional)
- Decorative fibers
- Silk flower
- Mini brad
- Desired embellishments
- Foam brush
- Craft knife
- Matte-finish preservative spray
- Decoupage medium
- Craft glue

Seashore Shaker

Design by SUSAN HUBER

A beautiful shoreline photo is the focal point of this mini frame. A dusting of mica flakes and glitter adds the look of shells in the surf.

MATERIALS
Seashore photo
Card stock:
blue-gray, white
Printable transparency
White foam-core board
White gel pen
Light blue chalk
Adhesive dots
Ultrafine
multicolored glitter
Pearlescent mica flakes
Gold shell charm
Iridescent white
craft thread
Craft knife
Large-eye needle
Craft cement
Glue stick
Double-sided tape
Foam tape
Alphabet rub-on
transfers (optional)
Computer with
fonts (optional)
Computer
printer (optional)

Cut a 5 x 3¾-inch piece of foam-core board with craft knife. ***Note:*** *Cut foam-core board in three steps: 1) Cut through top paper layer only. 2) Cutting in the same groove, cut through the foam layer only. 3) Cut the bottom paper layer.*

Cut a 4 x 2¾-inch piece from center, leaving a ½-inch-wide frame all around.

Cut two 5¼ x 3¾-inch pieces of blue-gray card stock. Cut a 3¾ x 2¼-inch piece from the center of *one* piece, leaving a ¾-inch-wide frame all around.

Cut a 5 x 3⅝-inch piece of white card stock. Cut a 3¾ x 2⅜-inch piece from center, leaving a ⅝-inch-wide frame all around.

Center and adhere white card stock frame to ¾-inch-wide blue-gray card stock frame with glue stick. Chalk the inner edges of the white frame.

Center and adhere photo to blue-gray card stock rectangle.

Use computer to generate, or hand-print, "Seashore" on printable transparency to fit within an area approximately 4 x 1 inches. Cut out word with craft knife; adhere to photo with adhesive dots. ***Option:*** *Use alphabet rub-on transfers.* Highlight word with white gel pen.

Adhere double-sided tape along all sides on back of foam-core frame. Peel off release strips; center and adhere foam-core frame to right side of photo.

Cut transparency slightly smaller than blue and white card-stock frame. Center and adhere transparency to back of card-stock frame with double-sided tape. Set aside.

Adhere double-sided tape along all sides on front of foam-core frame. Pour glitter and mica flakes onto photo inside foam-core frame. Peel off release strips; center and adhere card-stock frame to foam-core frame, capturing mica flakes and glitter inside.

Pierce small holes in upper corners of card-stock frame with large-eye needle. Thread white thread through holes; knot ends on front for hanger. Adhere seashell charm to lower right corner of frame with foam tape. ■

SOURCES: Charm from Westrim Crafts; mica flakes from USArtQuest.

Seashore

Good Friends

Design by BARBARA GREVE

Photos of special moments with siblings or friends framed with bright-colored papers transform wooden coasters into little works of art.

MATERIALS

- 4 (4¼-inch-square) wooden coasters
- Color copies of 4 color photos, each approximately 2½ x 2 inches
- Printed papers: bright pink, mango, turquoise and lime green, plus complementary multicolored patchwork
- Craft paints: bright pink, mango, turquoise, lime green
- Embroidery stitches rub-on transfers
- Mix-and-pour high-gloss finish
- 16 (½-inch) clear self-adhesive pads
- Fine sandpaper
- Damp cloth
- Foam brush
- Palette knife
- Laminating liquid

Paint each coaster a different color. Sand until smooth; wipe off dust. Apply a second coat of paint; let dry.

Center and adhere a 4-inch square of patchwork printed paper to each coaster with laminating liquid.

Measure photos; for each, cut a mat ¼ inch larger in each dimension from a printed paper to match coaster's paint. Adhere mats to coasters with laminating liquid; let dry. Center and adhere photos to mats with laminating liquid; let dry.

Apply embroidery stitch rub-on transfers to coasters, overlapping photos.

Following manufacturer's instructions, mix the high-gloss finish and pour over coasters, spreading finish evenly with a palette knife. Let coasters dry overnight.

Adhere self-adhesive pads to bottom of coasters. ■

SOURCES: Printed papers and rub-on transfers from K&Company; laminating liquid from Beacon; high-gloss finish from Environmental Technology Inc.

Mushroom Peg Board

Design by MARY AYRES

Sepia-toned nature photos teamed with a distressed peg board create a stunning home accent.

Paint peg board black. Sand surfaces and edges to give peg board a distressed look.

Trim photos to fit on front of peg board. Lightly sand edges of photos. Coat the backs of photos with permanent adhesive. Adhere photos to peg board.

Brush the photos and peg board with laminating liquid using the foam brush.

Use computer to generate, or hand-print, inspirational words onto white card stock to fit on small tags. Cut out words, leaving room on each tag to attach an eyelet. Punch a ⅛-inch hole in the end of each tag; set eyelets in holes.

Thread tags onto pieces of hemp cord; tie cords around peg board with knots on front, varying the positions of the tags. ***Option:*** *Adhere tags to peg board with dots of permanent adhesive.* ■

SOURCES: Peg board from Walnut Hollow; laminating liquid and permanent adhesive from Beacon.

MATERIALS

- 16¾ x 3½-inch wooden peg board
- Sepia-tone photos printed on no-sheen photo paper or presentation paper
- White card stock
- Black craft paint
- 6 (⅛-inch) antique eyelets
- Fine hemp cord
- 3-inch foam brush
- Fine sandpaper
- ⅛-inch hole punch
- Eyelet-setting tool
- Laminating liquid
- Permanent adhesive
- Computer with computer fonts (optional)

tea

Kitchen Tea Plaque

Design by SUSAN STRINGFELLOW

"Before" and "after" shots show one of the many ways to alter pictures using photo software.

MATERIALS

- 5¼ x 7¼-inch wooden plaque
- Photo on computer disk
- Pink gingham printed paper
- Matte-finish photo paper
- Foam stamps: decorative motif, alphabet
- Narrow blue rickrack
- 2 silk daisies
- Silk leaf
- Craft paints: white, pink, yellow
- Black ink pad
- Sawtooth hanger
- Foam brushes
- Indoor/outdoor gloss-finish varnish
- Decoupage medium
- Craft glue
- Computer with printer
- Image manipulation software

Paint outer edges of plaque pink; paint beveled edges yellow.

Cut pink gingham printed paper to fit on front of plaque; brush back of paper with decoupage medium. Press paper onto plaque, smoothing out wrinkles with your fingers.

Using image manipulation software, alter digital photo to desired effect. Print photo on matte-finish photo paper. Adhere photo to plaque near upper right corner with decoupage medium. Brush plaque with decoupage medium; let dry.

Stamp decorative motif off edge of plaque in lower left and upper right corners with white craft paint; repeat, stamping over white designs with yellow craft paint. Let dry.

Lightly ink edges and surface of plaque with black ink pad. Stamp "tea" on plaque in lower left corner with alphabet stamps and black paint. Let dry.

Brush entire plaque with two coats gloss-finish indoor/outdoor varnish.

Tie blue rickrack in a bow. Adhere bow, silk daisies and leaf in lower right corner of plaque with craft glue. Attach sawtooth hanger on back. ■

SOURCES: Plaque from Walnut Hollow; printed paper from My Mind's Eye; foam stamps from Making Memories; image manipulation software (Photoshop) Adobe; craft glue from Gorilla Glue.

Color My World

MATERIALS
- Blank CD
- Color photo
- Card stock: white, black, green
- Circle-cutting templates
- Foam brush
- Decoupage medium
- Computer with word processing and artistic programs
- Computer printer

Design by LINDA BEESON

Make easy work of this cute altered CD by using a circle template and a basic computer program.

Using computer, generate outlined letters to spell "you color my world" and arrange them in a 4⅜-inch circle, leaving a 2⁵⁄₁₆-inch circle blank in center for adding the photo later. Use computer program's art features to tint the letters in the colors of the rainbow. Print out on white card stock. Cut a 4⅜-inch circle around words.

Trace around CD onto black card stock; cut out. Center and adhere circle to CD with decoupage medium. Center and adhere lettered white circle to black circle with decoupage medium.

Cut a 2-inch circle around photo with circle-cutting template. Double-mat photo on a 2¼-inch circle cut from green card stock and a 2⅜-inch circle cut from black card stock, adhering with decoupage medium.

Adhere matted photo to center of lettered white circle with decoupage medium.

Brush front of CD, including photo, with several coats of decoupage medium. ■

SOURCES: Templates from AccuCut; computer programs from Microsoft; decoupage medium from Plaid.

Baseball Star

Design by SANDRA GRAHAM SMITH

Your little slugger will love this adorable shadow box that features him or her as the star of the game!

Cut a 4⅞ x 3⅞-inch piece of blue stars printed paper; adhere to mat board. Tear two irregular pieces of off-white script printed paper; adhere over blue stars printed paper. Adhere photo off to one side of layout.

Use computer to generate, or hand-print, baseball phrases in assorted fonts on white card stock or paper. Cut out phrases, trimming close to the letters. Arrange phrases and stickers on layout; adhere.

Cut strips of off-white script printed paper to fit on inside edges of frame; adhere to frame. Mount finished layout in frame. ■

MATERIALS

- 6¾ x 4¾-inch shadow-box frame
- 4⅞ x 3⅞-inch mat board
- Baseball photo *or* sports card
- White card stock *or* paper
- Printed papers: blue stars, off-white script
- Baseball stickers
- Glue stick
- Computer with computer fonts (optional)

Picture This

Design by NICOLE JACKSON

A computer-generated photo collage transforms a basic message board into a fun home accent.

MATERIALS

- 14 x 11-inch magnetic dry-erase board with memo magnets
- Photos on computer disk (optional)
- Photo paper (optional)
- Card stock
- Printed papers
- 1 yard satin ribbon
- 4 silk flowers
- 2 silver 5⁄16-inch brads
- Corner rounder punch
- Scrapbooking adhesive dots
- Adhesive dots
- Craft cement
- Computer with imaging software (optional)

Create a 7 x 10-inch photo collage with imaging software; print onto photo paper. ***Option:*** *Arrange actual photos in a collage; photocopy arrangement and trim to size.* Round upper left and lower left corners with corner rounder punch.

Cut 6½-inch strips of varying widths from a variety of printed papers. Adhere strips to a 6½ x 10-inch piece of card stock with adhesive dots, overlapping strips as desired. Round upper right and lower right corners with corner rounder punch.

Adhere scrapbooking adhesive dots to back of card stock. Press card stock with paper strips up against right edge of dry-erase board. ***Note***: *If the rounded corners do not match the corners of the dry-erase board precisely, slide the edges of the paper under the metal frame around the board until no dry-erase board is visible.*

Adhere photo collage to left side of dry-erase board with scrapbooking adhesive dots.

Cut two 18-inch pieces of ribbon. Adhere one end of each piece to back of board in an upper corner with craft cement; let dry for 24 hours. Tie ribbon ends in a bow; trim ends at an angle.

Magnets: Join two layers of silk flowers with a brad through their centers. Repeat with remaining flowers and brad. Adhere each flower/brad combo to one of the magnets that accompanied the dry-erase board with a dot of craft cement. ■

SOURCES: Dry-erase board and magnets from The Board Dudes; printed papers from Autumn Leaves; brads from Making Memories; craft cement from Eclectic Products.

My Boy

Design by SHERRY WRIGHT

MATERIALS

- 10 x 8-inch artist's canvas
- Photos
- Printed papers: blue, cream striped
- Alphabet stickers
- Alphabet rub-on transfers
- Light blue craft paint
- 1-inch-wide fabric strips *or* ribbons
- Foam brush
- Label maker with black label tape
- Staple gun
- Self-adhesive hook-and-loop tape
- Decoupage medium

Display favorite family photos on a canvas wall board decorated with paper and ribbons for an eye-catching piece of home decor.

Cut a 10 x 8-inch piece of blue printed paper and a 10 x 3¼-inch strip of cream striped printed paper; set aside. Paint edges of canvas light blue.

Coat front of canvas and back of blue printed paper with decoupage medium. Center and adhere paper to canvas, smoothing wrinkles with your fingers. Let dry.

Coat back of cream striped printed paper strip with decoupage medium. Adhere strip across front of canvas 1 inch from top. Let dry.

Cut a strip of hook-and-loop tape for each photo; adhere half of each strip to back of photo and the other half to the canvas. Press photos into place. ***Option:*** *Glue photos to canvas.*

Adhere alphabet stickers to cream striped printed paper strip in upper right corner to spell "BOY." Above stickers, apply alphabet rub-on tranfers to spell "My." Spell child's name on black label tape with label maker; adhere in lower left corner.

Hanger: Staple ends of assorted fabric strips to back of canvas in upper corners. Tie ends of fabric strips together in a large bow. ■

SOURCES: Printed papers and alphabet stickers from Imagination Project/Gin-X; rub-on transfers from Autumn Leaves; decoupage medium from Plaid.

Love Coasters

Design by SHERRY WRIGHT

Stoneware coasters embellished with photos and coordinating papers become a thoughtful gift for someone special.

Trace around coasters onto wrong side of printed papers; cut out. Brush backs of paper shapes and tops of coasters with decoupage medium. Press paper onto coasters, smoothing out wrinkles with your fingers. Let dry.

Trim photos to 2 inches square; round off corners with punch. Brush backs of photos with decoupage medium; adhere photos to coasters. Let dry.

Stamp coasters with flower images.

Cut separate letters from contrasting printed papers to spell "LOVE" with die-cutting machine and alphabet. Brush backs of letters with decoupage medium; adhere one letter to each coaster. ***Option:*** *Use alphabet stickers.*

Brush top of each coaster with a light coat of decoupage medium; let dry. Brush top of each coaster with several coats of decoupage medium, letting the medium dry between coats. ■

SOURCES: Coasters from Pfaltzgraf; printed papers from Chatterbox Inc.; rubber stamps from Close To My Heart; solvent-based inks from Tsukineko Inc.; die-cutting machine with dies from Sizzix/Ellison; decoupage medium from Plaid.

MATERIALS

4 stoneware coasters
4 photos
Printed papers
Flower stamps
Ink pads
Die-cutting machine with alphabet dies (optional)
Corner rounder punch
Foam brush
Decoupage medium

Forever Friends

Design by MARY AYRES

Personalize a glass candle shade with a favorite friendship photo and mulberry paper shapes—an ideal gift for yourself and a friend!

MATERIALS

- Candleholder with glass shade
- Black-and-white photo printed on no-sheen photo *or* presentation paper
- Pink card stock
- Mulberry paper: white, pink, turquoise, lime
- 3⁄16-inch turquoise eyelet
- ½-inch sheer light green pin-dot ribbon
- Self-adhesive pink rickrack
- White craft thread
- 3-inch foam brush
- Eyelet-setting tool
- 1¼-inch circle punch
- 3⁄16-inch hole punch
- Laminating liquid
- Gem glue
- Instant-dry paper glue
- Computer with computer fonts (optional)

Trim photo into a 2¼-inch circle. Adhere photo to glass lamp shade with gem glue.

Fold small squares of mulberry paper in half and then in quarters; cut designs in folded paper as if you were making paper snowflakes. Unfold; adhere shapes to lamp shade around photo with paper glue, centering some shapes on top of others and overlapping edges. ***Note:*** *Trim edges even with edges of lamp shade and photo.*

Brush lamp shade, including photo, with one coat of laminating liquid using a foam brush.

Adhere rickrack around edge of photo, butting ends neatly where they will be concealed by sheer ribbon bow.

Wrap sheer ribbon around shade near bottom, twisting it occasionally; tie ends in a bow at right side of photo.

Tag: Use computer to generate, or hand-print, "forever friends" on pink card stock. Punch words centered in a 1¼-inch circle. Punch a 3⁄16-inch hole near the top edge; set eyelet in hole. Tie tag to ribbon bow with white craft thread. ■

SOURCES: Rickrack from Colorbök; laminating liquid, gem glue and instant-dry paper glue from Beacon.

forever
friends

CARDS & TAGS

Nothing is more personal than a handmade card or tag to accompany a special gift. Add a photo and you've created something even warmer and more personal.

Missing You

Design by SUSAN STRINGFELLOW

The "missing you" sentiment combines with a photo of sad puppy-dog eyes to succinctly state your thoughts.

MATERIALS

- Photo of puppy
- Card stock: neutral, black
- Neutral diamond-pattern printed paper
- Neutral fabric paper
- Decorative rub-on transfer
- Ink: linen, black
- Fine sandpaper
- Glue stick
- Computer with computer fonts (optional)
- Computer printer (optional)

Cut a 7 x 10-inch piece of card stock; fold in half to form a 7 x 5-inch card with fold at top. Ink edges of card with linen and black inks.

Cut a 6¾ x 4¾-inch piece of printed paper. Sand the edges and ink with linen ink. Center and adhere printed paper to card.

Trim photo to 5⅞ x 3⅞ inches. Mat photo on black card stock; trim, leaving narrow border. Center and adhere photo to card.

Use computer to print "missing you" three times on fabric paper to fit on a strip 5 x ½ inch; trim strip to size and adhere up left edge of card. ***Option:*** *Letter fabric paper by hand with a black permanent fine-tip marker, or use black alphabet rub-on transfers.*

Apply decorative rub-on transfer to lower right corner of card, overlapping photo. ■

SOURCES: Printed paper from The Paper Loft; fabric paper from me & my BIG ideas; rub-on transfer from Heidi Swapp/Advantus Corp.; inks from Ranger Industries and Tsukineko Inc.

Explore Nature

Design by SUSAN HUBER

A mini accordion-fold photo book is the highlight on the cover of a card designed with an appreciation for nature.

MATERIALS

- 2-inch-square "Explore" magnetic accordion-fold book
- 2-inch-square photos
- Card stock: solid moss green, green/brown/blue/cream striped, blue-green
- 1⅞ x 2¼-inch "N" stencil
- Printable transparency
- "Ocean" transparency
- Black distress ink
- Decorative fibers and ribbons
- Glue stick
- Foam tape
- Clear adhesive dots
- Computer with fonts (optional)
- Computer printer (optional)

Cut an 11 x 4¼-inch strip of moss green card stock; score and fold in half to form a 5½ x 4¼-inch card with fold on left edge. Cut a 5 x 3¾-inch piece of striped card stock; center and adhere to front of card. Wrap fibers around cover of card near spine; knot at top of card.

Punch out "N" stencil. Reassemble punched-out pieces on a 1⅞ x 2½-inch piece of blue-green card stock; adhere with glue stick. Heavily ink edges of card stock and lightly ink surface of "N" with distress ink. Adhere "N" panel to front of card at an angle with foam tape.

Use computer to generate, or hand-print, "ATURE" on printable transparency to fit within an area approximately 3 x ¾ inch. ***Option:*** *Use alphabet rub-on transfers.* Trim transparency to 3⅝ x 1⅝ inches; adhere to front of card with adhesive dots to complete the word "NATURE."

Adhere photos to pages of accordion-fold book with glue stick; adhere "Ocean" transparency to one page with adhesive dots. ■

SOURCES: Card stock from Die Cuts With A View; magnetic book from Karen Foster Design; "Ocean" transparency from Design Originals; distress ink from Ranger Industries.

Snowmobiling Dad

Design by LORINE MASON

Paper weaving turns a colored photo reprint into a card designed to honor Dad.

Cut a 12 x 6¼-inch piece of textured red card stock; score and fold in half to form a 6 x 6¼-inch card with fold on left edge.

Trim photo to fit on front of card. Mark vertical center of photo. Measuring outward, mark photo into five vertical sections. They need not be exactly even; be sure to leave main image intact.

Cut photo apart along lines. Glue top edge of each strip to front of card.

Cut several ¹⁄₁₆-inch-wide strips from textured red card stock. Weave red strips through the photo strips as shown without obscuring the main image. Trim ends of strips and adhere to front of card with paper glue.

Adhere bottom edge of photo strips to front of card. Frame photo with ¼-inch-wide strips cut from black card stock; adhere with paper glue. Punch ¹⁄₁₆-inch holes in corners of frame; mount mini brads in holes.

Adhere letter tiles to front of card with adhesive foam squares. ■

MATERIALS

- Copy of color photo
- Card stock: textured red, black
- Square alphabet tiles to spell "DAD"
- 4 nickle mini brads
- ¹⁄₁₆-inch hole punch
- Paper glue
- Adhesive foam squares

MATERIALS

- Small black-and-white photos
- Card stock: white, pastel green, pink, blue, yellow
- Pastel printed papers: florals, plaids
- Small silver frames and/or photo corners
- Black inspirational-themed word rub-on transfers
- Pink ink pad
- Pastel fibers
- Sheer white wire-edge ribbon
- Dry sponge
- ¼-inch hole punch
- Instant-dry paper glue

Inspirational Tags

Designs by MARY AYRES

Quick and easy to make, these lovely tags will remind you of the simple joys of life.

Project note: *Ink edges of all papers and card stocks except photos with pink ink pad and dry sponge.*

Cut a 6 x 3-inch tag from pastel green card stock. Cut a 4¾ x 2¾-inch piece of printed paper; adhere to square end of tag ⅛ inch from edges.

Transfer word rub-on onto pink, blue or yellow card stock; trim rectangle around word, leaving more space on the left side. Mat rectangle on white card stock; trim, leaving a ⅛-inch white border.

Punch a ¼-inch hole in left end of rectangle. Thread sheer white ribbon through hole and wrap ribbon around tag, tying ends in front. Position rectangle toward left end of printed paper rectangle; adhere.

Trim photo to fit in frame or photo corners; adhere photo and frame (or corners) to bottom right corner of tag.

Cut a ⅜-inch square of white card stock; center and adhere to left end of tag. Punch a ¼-inch hole through center of square. Thread 10-inch lengths of fiber through hole; knot. ■

SOURCES: Printed papers from K&Company; instant-dry paper glue from Beacon.

Hosta Card

Design by MARY AYRES

Pair a black-and-white print with the same photo printed in color to create an eye-catching card.

MATERIALS

- 4 x 6-inch high-contrast black-and-white photo
- Same photo printed in color in wallet size
- Card stock: khaki, white
- 1 1/2 x 1 7/8-inch silver oval frame with eyelet
- Silver eyelets: 12 (3/16-inch), 1 (1/8-inch)
- Fine cord: black leather, hemp
- Hole punches: 1/8-inch, 3/16-inch
- Eyelet-setting tool
- Sewing machine with black thread
- Spray preservative
- Instant-dry paper glue
- Computer with computer fonts (optional)

Cut a 10 x 8-inch piece of khaki card stock; score and fold to form a 5 x 8-inch card with fold at left.

Spray all photos with preservative. Cut black-and-white photo into six 4 x 1-inch strips. Adhere strips, evenly spaced, to front of card. Machine-stitch around front of card 1/8 inch from edge using black thread and a straight stitch; machine-stitch down long edges of card a second time, 5/8 inch from edge, over short ends of photo strips.

Punch six 3/16-inch holes down sides of card, opposite centers of photo strips. Set 3/16 inch eyelets in holes. Weave hemp cord in and out of eyelets on one side of card. Weave a second piece of hemp cord back through the same holes in the opposite direction; knot ends of cords together at top and bottom; trim ends. Repeat on reverse side of card.

Use computer to generate, or hand-print, "hostas" on white card stock to fit in an area about 5/8 inch wide. Trim a small pointed tag shape around word. Punch a 1/8-inch hole in end of tag; set 1/8-inch eyelet in hole. Tie tag to eyelet in oval frame with fine black leather cord.

Trim color photo to fit in oval frame; adhere photo in frame. Adhere frame and tag to card. ■

SOURCES: Frame from Nunn Design; spray preservative from Krylon; instant-dry paper glue from Beacon.

4th of JULY

Festive Fireworks

Design by SUSAN HUBER

Celebrate our nation's independence with a star-spangled card featuring a fun family photo.

Cut an 11 x 5½-inch piece of blue card stock; score and fold in half to form a 5½-inch-square card with fold on left edge. Ink edges with distress ink.

Cut a 2 x 5-inch strip of red printed paper; adhere to front of card near left edge with glue stick. Cut a 3¼ x 1½-inch strip of blue printed paper; adhere near bottom edge with glue stick.

Use a computer to generate, or hand-print, "celebrate" on printable transparency to fit within an area approximately 4½ x ⅞ inch. ***Option:*** *Use alphabet rub-on transfers.* Trim transparency to 4⅞ x 1⅛ inches; adhere to red printed paper rectangle on card front with adhesive dots.

Center and adhere "Independence" sticker to blue printed paper rectangle at bottom of card. Adhere acrylic stars to card, overlapping sticker, with craft cement.

Adhere family photo to red card stock with glue stick; trim around photo, leaving narrow border. Repeat, adhering matted photo to blue card stock. Adhere matted photo to front of card with two hinges and craft cement. Attach 4th of July fabric tab to right edge of photo.

Open photo by hinges. Cover back of photo panel with a piece of blue printed paper cut to size; add a round red star sticker.

Cut blue printed paper to fit on card front behind family photo; adhere with glue stick. Mat fireworks photo on red card stock; cut out, leaving a narrow border. Adhere matted photo to blue printed paper behind family photo panel. Add a white star sticker over lower left corner of fireworks photo.

Attach small strips of hook-and-loop tape to back of fabric tab and corresponding spot on edge of card front. ■

SOURCES: Printed papers, stickers and fabric tab from Scrapworks; hinges from Making Memories; acrylic stars from LazerLetterz; distress ink from Ranger Industries.

MATERIALS

- 2 photos: 3⅜ x 2⅝-inch photo of family; 2 x 2⅜-inch photo of fireworks
- Card stock: red, blue
- Printed papers: red, white and blue stars and starbursts
- Printable transparency
- Red, white and blue "Independence" and round star stickers
- Dark red distress ink
- 2 (¾-inch) hinges
- Red acrylic stars
- "4th of July" fabric tab
- Self-adhesive hook-and-loop tape
- Glue stick
- Craft cement
- Computer with fonts (optional)
- Computer printer (optional)

Have a Ball

MATERIALS

- Photo
- Red card stock
- Printed papers: red striped, blue mottled
- Plain white paper
- 4 (⅝-inch-diameter) bubble stickers
- Glue stick
- Computer with computer fonts (optional)

Design by SANDRA GRAHAM SMITH

A brightly colored photo personalizes this fun and festive birthday card!

Cut a 5½ x 8½-inch piece of red card stock; score and fold in half to form a 5½ x 4¼-inch card with fold on top edge.

Cut a 4 x 4¼-inch piece of red striped printed paper; adhere to front of card ½ inch from left side.

Cut four 1 x 3¾-inch strips of blue mottled printed paper. Center and adhere one strip ⅛ inch from fold and from left edge. Repeat along right edge. Adhere remaining strips near right-hand strip, ⅛ inch apart.

Trim photo to 3¾ x 3⅛ inches; adhere to front of card 1 inch from left edge.

Cut two ⅝-inch circles from red striped printed paper and two from red card stock. Adhere bubble stickers over circles. Center and adhere circles down left-hand blue strip.

Use computer to generate, or hand-print, "Happy Birthday Have a Ball!" on white paper to fit within an area approximately 2½ x ½ inch. Trim lettering strip to 4½ x 1 inch; adhere over lower right corner of card. Trim strip even with edges of card.

Embellish envelope as desired with strips and circles cut from printed papers and card stock. ■

SOURCES: Printed papers from Provo Craft and Die Cuts With A View.

We're Moving

Design by MARY LYNN MALONEY

A pocket card made with bubble wrap is the ideal way to announce your move. Tuck a card inside with your new address information.

MATERIALS
- 5 x 7-inch cardboard
- Photos
- Green card stock
- Blue mulberry paper
- Plain white paper
- Large manila tag
- Bubble wrap
- Alphabet stamps
- Red ink pad
- Fine hemp twine
- Craft knife
- Brown packing tape
- Glue stick
- Computer with computer fonts (optional)

Cut 5 x 7-inch piece of bubble wrap; trim off one upper corner at an angle to create pocket. Affix bubble wrap to front of cardboard with brown packing tape along side and bottom edges, smoothing edges of tape onto back.

Stamp "We Are Moving" on blue mulberry paper to fit within an area approximately 2 x ⅝ inch. Trim around lettering. Center and adhere lettering to 4¼ x 1½-inch strip of green card stock; tear card stock along long edges. Adhere card stock across bottom of pocket with glue stick; adhere additional packing tape over the corners.

Tag: Stamp "Our New Address" at top of tag. Tear bottom edge off tag. Cut and tear 3½ x 2½-inch piece of blue mulberry paper; adhere to tag. Cut and tear a 3 x 1½-inch piece of green card stock; adhere to blue mulberry paper.

Use computer to generate, or hand-print, name and new address on white paper; trim to fit on green card stock; adhere with glue stick.

Affix brown packing tape over the right edge of tag, overlapping address panel. Thread hemp cord through hole in tag.

Slip photos of new home into pocket behind bubble wrap. Slip address tag behind photos. ■

Relax Card

Design by MARY AYRES

Create a simple but stylish greeting card using mirror-image photos.

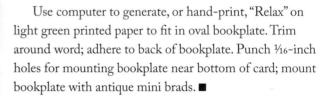

MATERIALS
- 2 x 3-inch color photos: 2 of the same subject, 2 of the same subject printed in mirror image
- Black card stock
- Printed papers: light green, dark green
- 1¾-inch silver oval bookplate
- Brads: decorative square, 2 antique mini
- Fine sandpaper
- Hole punches: ⅛-inch, 1⁄16-inch
- Sewing machine with black thread
- Instant-dry paper glue
- Computer with computer fonts (optional)

Cut a 10 x 8-inch piece of black card stock; score and fold to form a 5 x 8-inch card with fold at left.

Cut a 4¾ x 6½-inch piece of dark green printed paper; sand edges and glue to front of card ⅛ inch from top edge.

Lightly draw a horizontal line across center of dark green printed paper; draw another line down vertical center. Machine-stitch over lines to edges of dark green printed paper using black thread and a straight stitch.

Sand edges of photos. Adhere photos in mirror-image positions inside stitched quadrants.

Punch a ⅛-inch hole in center of photo panel; mount decorative brad in hole.

Use computer to generate, or hand-print, "Relax" on light green printed paper to fit in oval bookplate. Trim around word; adhere to back of bookplate. Punch 1⁄16-inch holes for mounting bookplate near bottom of card; mount bookplate with antique mini brads. ■

SOURCES: Printed papers from Basic Grey; instant-dry paper glue from Beacon.

Get Away

Design by LINDA BEESON

Digital photography and photo-editing programs open up a whole new world for creating unique photo greeting cards!

Cut a 5¼ x 10½-inch piece of textured black card stock; score and fold in half to form a 5¼-inch-square card with fold at top. Cut a 4⅜ x 5¼-inch piece of road trip printed paper; adhere to front of card near left edge.

Alter photo as desired on computer. ***Note:*** *Sample is a photo of a painted sign, altered with a "painting" effect in a photo-editing program.*

Size photo to 3⅜ x 4¾ inches; print onto photo paper and cut out. Round off corners with corner punch; sand edges of photo.

Mat photo onto textured rust card stock; cut around photo leaving a ⅛-inch border. Adhere matted photo to front of card as shown.

Paint each chipboard tile a different color; let dry. Stamp travel words on tiles with alphabet stamps and black pigment ink; let dry. Coat each tile with lacquer; let dry. Adhere tiles to card. ■

SOURCES: Printed paper from Sticker Studio; stamps from FontWerks; solvent-based ink from Tsukineko; clear lacquer from Sakura.

MATERIALS

- Travel-themed digital photo
- Textured card stock: black, rust
- "Road trip" printed paper
- Double-sided matte-finish photo paper
- 3 (1¾ x ⅝-inch) chipboard tiles
- ¼-inch alphabet stamps
- Black pigment ink pad
- Craft paints: pink, yellow, light brown
- Fine sandpaper
- Paintbrush
- Corner rounder punch
- Clear lacquer
- Double-sided tape
- Computer with photo and artistic programs (optional)
- Computer printer (optional)

Matchbook Card

Design by SHERRY WRIGHT

This card, designed with grandparents in mind, opens up to reveal a sweet-surprise photo book!

Project note: *Adhere all elements with double-sided tape unless instructed otherwise.*

Cut a 5 x 9-inch piece of burgundy card stock; score and fold in half to form a 5 x 4½-inch card with fold at top.

Cover: Cut a piece of striped printed paper slightly smaller than front of card; adhere to front of card.

Adhere grandparents-themed vellum across top of card. Thread buckle slide onto ribbon; adhere ribbon and slide to front of card near bottom with adhesive dots. Wrap ribbon ends around to back; adhere.

Inside: Cut striped printed paper to cover inside of card front; adhere.

Cut a 3 x 7½-inch strip of burgundy card stock; score and fold at 3, 3¼ and 7 inches to form a large matchbook. Cut a 2⅞-inch square of blocks printed paper; adhere to matchbook cover.

With label maker, print grandchild's name, "HUGS AND KISSES," "YOU," "LOVE," "FOR YOU" and "OPEN" on black tape. Adhere "OPEN" to bottom strip of matchbook cover.

Cut a 2¾ x 10¼-inch strip of cream card stock; score and fold strip accordion-style, making first fold ¼ inch from top, and remaining folds every 2½ inches.

Trim photos to fit on accordion panels. Reserve "YOU" label; adhere remaining labels to photo panels as desired. On last panel (adjacent to ¼-inch tab), adhere "I love you" message, applying "I" rub-on transfer at top left, adhering heart die cut to center, and "You" label in lower right corner.

Adhere top ¼-inch flap of accordion strip to back of matchbook. Adhere matchbook inside card.

Envelope: Form cream card stock into a 6-inch-square envelope with envelope template. Fold together and adhere.

Embellish front and back of envelope as desired with strips and squares of printed paper and labels made with label maker. ■

SOURCES: Printed papers from Daisy D's Paper Co.; vellum from All My Memories; die cut from QuicKutz; buckle slide from Nunn Design; envelope template from Green Sneakers Inc.

MATERIALS

- Small photos of grandchild
- Card stock: burgundy, cream
- Printed papers: multicolor striped, number/letter blocks
- Grandparents-themed self-adhesive vellum
- 1⅝ x ⅝-inch buckle slide
- ⅝-inch-wide brown grosgrain ribbon
- "I" rub-on transfer
- Red heart die cut
- Label maker with black label tape
- Template for 6-inch-square envelope
- Adhesive dots
- Double-sided adhesive tape

MATERIALS

- White 6¼ x 5-inch card with fold at top
- Digital photos on computer
- Photo paper
- Card stock: white, blue
- Printed papers: blue/green polka dot, striped, plaid, gingham checked
- White mini brads
- Decorative punches: tag, teddy bear
- Decorative-edge scissors
- 1⁄16-inch hole punch
- Glue stick
- Dimensional adhesive foam dot
- Digital imaging software
- Computer with printer

Baby Welcome

Designs by JACQUELINE JONES

Turn photos of your new bundle of joy into adorable baby announcements with your computer and digital image software.

Use computer program to crop photos to approximately 4⅜ x 2 inches and soften edges. Above photos, create rectangles and fill with blue. Add "welcome"; fill text with white. Superimpose baby's name over top edge of photos; fill text with blue.

Print photos with "welcome" panels on desired photo paper leaving 1⁄16-inch white border all around. ***Option:*** *Crop existing photos; mount on blue card stock to create the color-block effect. Transfer "welcome" and name with blue and white alphabet rub-on transfers or rubber stamps.*

Continuing with instructions for individual card, mount photo on white card stock with glue stick. Tear card-stock edges around photo.

Cut two pieces of complementary printed paper 5⅞ x 2½ inches; adhere to front of card, overlapping edges and leaving narrow border all around.

Cut narrow blue card-stock strip with decorative-edge scissors; adhere across card over seam between printed papers. Adhere photo to card front at an angle.

Punch matching teddy bear shapes from blue card stock and white card stock; punch matching tag shapes from printed paper and white card stock. Adhere matching shapes together with glue stick, offsetting them slightly.

Adhere teddy bear to tag. Punch 1⁄16-inch hole in top of tag; mount white mini brad in hole. Adhere tag to front of card with dimensional adhesive foam dot. ■

SOURCE: Digital imaging software from Microsoft.

Daddy's Little Girl

Design by SANDRA GRAHAM SMITH

A priceless father-and-daughter photo tucked inside a pocket card will melt any daddy's heart.

Pocket: Using pattern provided (page 159), trace library pocket onto cream flecked card stock. Cut out; score along dashed lines with stylus. Fold tabs in and adhere to form pocket. Punch upper corners with lacy corner punch.

Cut a 3½-inch square of light blue card stock. Cut a 3½ x 3¼-inch piece of cream floral printed paper; center and adhere to light blue card stock.

Tear adhered pieces in half down the center. Punch five matching 1/16-inch holes, evenly spaced, down torn edge of each piece. Thread gold cord through holes to join pieces shoelace-style; tie ends in a bow at the top. Adhere entire piece to front of pocket.

Photo card: Cut a 3¼ x 5½-inch piece of light blue card stock; punch all corners with lacy corner punch.

Cut a 2¾ x 4½-inch piece of cream floral printed paper; punch all corners with lacy corner punch. Center and adhere floral printed paper to light blue card stock.

Using pattern provided (page 159), cut photo in the shape of a heart; adhere to photo card.

Use computer to generate, or hand-print, family- and dad-themed sayings on white paper. Trim; adhere sayings to pocket and photo card. Slip photo card into pocket. ■

SOURCE: Corner punch from Fiskars.

PATTERNS ON PAGE 159

MATERIALS

- Photo
- Card stock: cream flecked, solid light blue
- Cream floral printed paper
- Plain white paper
- Fine gold metallic cord
- Lacy corner punch
- 1/16-inch hole punch
- Stylus
- Glue stick
- Computer with computer fonts (optional)

Lovely Ladies

Designs by KATHY WEGNER

Heritage photos and antique-looking embellishments create cards with a vintage look.

MATERIALS

- 2 (5 x 7-inch) blank ivory greeting cards with envelopes
- 2 black-and-white photos
- Black card stock
- Printed papers: black-and-cream floral, cream floral
- Tan vellum
- Black adhesive mesh
- Rubber stamps: "I love you dearly," "I miss you"
- Black dye ink pad
- 12 black mini brads
- Bone folder
- Decorative-edge scissors
- 1/16-inch "anywhere" hole punch *or* large needle
- Double-sided adhesive sheets
- Clear *or* white mounting tabs

For each card, stamp selected sentiment on cream floral printed paper with black dye ink.

Adhere vellum on top of photo with double-sided adhesive sheet. Burnish vellum to photo with bone folder. Trim photo to 2½ x 3¾ inches with decorative-edge scissors.

Using decorative-edge scissors throughout, trim black card stock slightly larger than photo. Trim black-and-cream floral printed paper to approximately 3¼ x 4½ inches. Center and adhere photo to black card stock, and then black card stock to floral printed paper with mounting tabs.

Trim around stamped sentiment, then trim black-and-cream floral printed paper slightly larger. Center and adhere sentiment to floral printed paper with mounting tabs.

Cut a 3⅝ x 7-inch piece of black adhesive mesh; center and adhere to front of card. Punch 1/16-inch hole in each corner of black-and-cream floral printed paper on photo panel and in center on each side of black-and-cream floral printed paper on sentiment panel. Punch matching holes through front of card. Mount photo and sentiment to card with black mini brads.

Envelope: Adhere double-sided adhesive sheet to wrong side of black-and-cream floral printed paper. Cut a 1 x 5¼-inch strip from floral printed paper; trim long edges with decorative-edge scissors. Adhere strip up left side of envelope close to edge. ■

SOURCES: Anna Griffin rubber stamps from Plaid; adhesive sheets and mounting tabs from Therm O Web.

I love you dearly
I Miss YOU

Elegant Ancestors

Designs by KATHY WEGNER

Attach vintage-look gift tags to an elegantly wrapped package for a lovely gift set.

MATERIALS

- Copies of vintage photos
- Card stock: gold and silver metallic or foil; white or ivory
- Plain white paper
- ¼-inch eyelets: gold, silver
- Metallic ribbon or cord: 12 inches each gold, silver
- Silver heart clip
- Very fine silver wire
- Mini brads: 2 gold, 4 silver
- Decorative punches: butterfly, heart
- Pattern-tracing wheel
- Hole punches: 1⁄16-inch, 3⁄16-inch
- Eyelet-setting tool
- Cutting mat
- Double-sided adhesive sheet
- 3⁄16-inch adhesive dots

GOLD TAG

Cut a pattern for a 3⅛ x 6¼-inch tag shape from plain white paper. Trace around pattern onto back of gold card-stock; cut out.

Lay card-stock tag right side down on cutting mat. Roll tracing wheel over back of tag to add desired pattern. Punch a 3⁄16-inch hole near top of tag; set gold eyelet in hole.

Adhere photo to white or ivory card stock with double-sided adhesive sheet. Trim photo to fit on tag. Adhere photo to tag with adhesive dots.

Punch 1⁄16-inch holes through photo and tag; attach gold mini brads through holes.

Punch six butterflies from scraps of gold card stock; adhere to tag with adhesive dots. Fold gold ribbon or cord in half; thread through eyelet.

SILVER TAG

Follow instructions for gold tag, substituting silver materials and heart decorative punch. Wire silver heart clip to mini brad in corner of photo. ■

SOURCE: Decorative punches from EK Success.

Heritage Tag

Design by SANDRA GRAHAM SMITH

A vintage-style frame surrounds an heirloom photo, making this tag a family keepsake.

Using pattern provided (page 160), cut tag from olive green card stock. Punch a ⅛-inch hole near top edge; set eyelet in hole. Thread tassel through eyelet.

Using pattern provided (page 160), cut a tag envelope from green floral printed paper; score along dashed line and fold front up.

Cut a piece of pink floral printed paper to cover front of envelope, positioning pink/green stripes in paper along left edge. Adhere paper to front of envelope.

Punch five ⅛-inch holes evenly spaced down left edge of envelope through all layers; set eyelets in holes. Punch ⅛-inch hole in each corner of envelope on right edge through all layers; set eyelets in holes.

Trim photo to fit in frame; adhere frame and photo to front of envelope.

Punch edge on a strip of green floral printed paper with lace punch; adhere across bottom of tag. Trim pink/green stripes from pink floral paper, adhere across top of lace-edged strip.

Adhere envelope to tag with double-sided adhesive.

Card: Cut a 1⅞ x 3¼-inch piece of pink floral printed paper, a 1⅝ x 3-inch piece of olive green card stock, and a 1⅜ x 2¾-inch piece of green floral printed paper. Center pieces on one another to layer; adhere with glue stick. Punch a key from olive green card stock; adhere to card with glue stick.

Stamp words onto pink floral printed paper with black ink. Cut tiny rectangles around words; adhere to card with glue stick. Tuck card into envelope. ■

SOURCES: Anna Griffin printed paper from Plaid; stamp from Mrs. O'Leary's/Artful Illusions; punches from The Punch Bunch and Fiskars; double-sided adhesive sheet from Therm O Web.

PATTERNS ON PAGE 160

MATERIALS

- Photo
- Olive green card stock
- Printed papers: pink floral with pink/green stripe, green floral
- Heritage-themed word rubber stamp
- Black ink pad
- 2-inch gold metal heart frame with pearl
- 8 (⅛-inch) gold eyelets
- Pink tassel
- Punches: lace edge, key
- ⅛-inch hole punch
- Eyelet-setting tool
- Glue stick
- Double-sided adhesive sheet

MATERIALS
- Close-up digital photo of gift ribbons on package
- Textured white card stock
- Printed papers: red polka dot, purple striped
- Double-sided matte-finish photo paper
- Lavender ink pad
- Numeral sticker
- Fine sandpaper
- Corner rounder punch
- Double-sided tape
- Computer with photo and artistic programs (optional)
- Computer printer (optional)

Happy Birthday to You!

Design by LINDA BEESON

A digital close-up photo of ribbons on a gift package becomes the focal point of this fun birthday card.

Cut a 5¼ x 10½-inch piece of textured white card stock; score and fold in half to form a 5¼-inch-square card with fold at top. Ink edges with lavender ink pad. Cut triangles from red polka-dot printed paper; adhere to corners on front of card.

On computer, print "Happy Birthday to You" in white ("no color" option) on photo. Size photo to 3⅞ inches square; print onto photo paper and cut out. ***Option:*** *Add lettering to photo with white rub-on transfers, or alphabet stamps and white paint.* Round off corners with corner punch. Sand edges of photo.

Cut a 4¾-inch square of purple striped printed paper; round off corners with corner punch. Center and adhere photo to purple square; adhere square to front of card. Adhere numeral sticker in lower right corner. ■

SOURCE: Printed papers from Making Memories.

Seeking

Design by EILEEN HULL

Turn an inspirational sentiment and the photo of an interesting door into a unique greeting card.

Cut an 8½ x 6½-inch piece of tan card stock; score and fold in half to form a 4¼ x 6½-inch card with fold on left edge.

Cut a piece of blue card stock approximately 4¼ x 2½ inches; tear top and bottom edges. Stipple edges with light brown paint and stencil brush.

Use computer to generate, or hand-print, "knock … and it will be opened to you. Matthew 7:7" on tan card stock to fit within an area approximately 2⅜ x 1 inch; trim strip to 4¼ x 2 inches, centering words; tear top and bottom edges. Stipple edges with light brown paint and stencil brush.

Use computer to generate, or hand-print, "ask, knock, seek, ask, knock, seek" in a column on tan card stock to fit inside door in photo.

Mat photo on plain tan card stock; cut around door on three sides with craft knife so that it can be folded open; lay photo on printed tan card stock, checking that "ask, knock, seek …" is framed in doorway. Adhere edges of photo to card stock with spray adhesive, avoiding door and printed area. Trim edges of card-stock pieces even with photo.

Mat photo/printed card-stock assembly on light brown card stock; trim around assembly, leaving a ⅛-inch border.

Layer torn blue card stock strip on front of card, then "Matthew 7:7" tan card stock strip; adhere with spray adhesive, leaving center top portion of tan card stock strip free. Set snaps in ends of strips.

Slide bottom edge of matted photo between tan and blue card stock strips; adhere photo to card with double-sided tape.

Shade edges of card with stencil brush and light brown paint, swirling brush lightly in a circular motion. ■

SOURCE: Spray adhesive from Krylon.

MATERIALS

- Photo of colorful doorway, approximately 2¼ x 3½ inches
- Card stock: tan, blue, light brown
- Light brown craft paint
- 2 light brown snaps
- Snap-setting tool
- Craft knife
- Stencil brush
- Spray adhesive
- Double-sided adhesive tape
- Computer with computer fonts (optional)
- Computer printer (optional)

Live, Laugh, Love

Design by MARY AYRES

Spread some cheer and good wishes when you send this card embellished with photos of bright summer blossoms.

MATERIALS

- 3 color photos of flowers, at least 1½ inches square, printed on no-sheen photo paper
- 3 color photos of grass or grasslike plants, at least 1½ x 2¾ inches, printed on regular photo paper
- Card stock: dark brown, white
- Brown corrugated paper
- Ink pads: blue, green, brown
- 3 (1½-inch) clear adhesive-backed disks
- 3 (2 x 3½-inch) distressed tags
- 6 (³⁄₁₆-inch) silver eyelets
- 6 screw-top silver mini brads
- 3 brown buttons
- Strands of black burlap
- Fine hemp cord
- Dry sponge
- Fine sandpaper
- Hole punches: ¹⁄₁₆-inch, ³⁄₁₆-inch
- Eyelet-setting tool
- Instant-dry paper glue
- Computer with computer fonts (optional)

Cut a 7½ x 10-inch piece of brown card stock; score and fold to form a 7½ x 5-inch card with fold at top.

Cut three ¾-inch squares from brown corrugated paper; rub surfaces with brown ink and dry sponge. Adhere squares, evenly spaced, across top of card. Thread hemp cord through holes in buttons; knot ends on top of buttons. Adhere buttons to corrugated squares.

Sand edges of tags. Punch two ³⁄₁₆-inch holes ¾ inch apart in top of each tag. Set eyelets in holes.

Cut three 1½ x 2¾-inch rectangles from grass photos; ink edges with green ink pad and dry sponge. Center and adhere a grass photo to each tag.

Adhere clear disks to flower photos; trim photo edges even with disks. Adhere disks to tags as shown.

Use computer to generate, or hand-print, "LIVE," "LAUGH" and "LOVE" on white card stock to fit within strips approximately 3 x ⅜ inch. Cut strips around words; ink edges with blue ink. Glue strips across tags at angles; trim ends even with tags. Punch ¹⁄₁₆-inch holes in ends of strips; mount mini brads in holes.

Thread burlap strands through eyelets on tags and wrap around buttons. Adhere tags to card at angles. ■

SOURCE: Instant-dry paper glue from Beacon.

LIVE
LAUGH
LOVE

Bird-Nest Photo Card

Design by KATHLEEN PANEITZ

A close-up photo of a nest full of newly laid eggs is ideal for a spring welcome card.

MATERIALS

- 3½ x 5-inch printed card-stock bird nest frame
- Close-up photo of eggs in nest
- Pink card stock
- Tiny white "spring" card-stock tag
- Rub-on alphabet transfers to spell "happy"
- ⅜-inch-wide cream grosgrain ribbon with pink polka dots
- Adhesive

Cut a 7¼ x 5¼-inch piece of pink card stock; score and fold in half to form a 3⅝ x 5¼-inch card with fold on left edge.

Trim photo to fit behind bird-nest frame, positioning image of nest with eggs in frame opening; adhere photo to wrong side of frame. Center and adhere frame and photo to front of card.

Transfer letters to spell "happy" to lower left quadrant of frame. Knot ribbon through hole in "spring" tag; trim ribbon ends at an angle. Adhere tag and ribbon to card to right of "happy" transfer. ■

SOURCES: Frame from Anna Griffin Inc.; tag from Making Memories; rub-on transfers from 7gypsies; ribbon from K&Company.

Man's Best Friend

Design by KATHLEEN PANEITZ

Open the chipboard flap on this tag to reveal a photo of the cherished four-legged member of your family!

MATERIALS

- "Dog" chipboard coaster
- Photo
- Card stock: rust, brown, light blue striped
- "little one" tag
- Rub-on transfers: letters, numbers
- Paw-print rubber stamp
- Sepia ink pad
- Hinge
- Dog-themed printed twill tape
- Paw-print ribbon
- ¼-inch hole punch
- Double-sided tape

Cut a 5⅜ x 4⅛-inch tag from light blue striped card stock; center and punch a ¼-inch hole in end.

Trim photo to fit on striped tag. Adhere photo to brown card stock. Trim around photo, leaving a narrow border. Adhere to striped tag. Transfer date, age, etc., to brown and rust card stocks; trim and adhere to striped tag.

Tie "little one" tag over photo through hole in striped tag with paw-print ribbon.

Stamp paw prints on back of coaster with sepia ink. Transfer dog's name to back of coaster with alphabet rub-ons.

Cut a 2-inch strip of printed twill tape; fold in half. Apply double-sided tape across ends; sandwich edge of coaster between ends of twill tape and press to adhere, forming a twill tab.

Adhere chipboard coaster to right edge of striped tag with metal hinge, stamped paw prints facing photo. ■

SOURCES: Coaster from Cloud 9 Design; card stock and tag from My Mind's Eye; rub-on transfers from Autumn Leaves; rubber stamp from Delta/Rubber Stampede; ink pad from Ranger Industries; hinge from Making Memories; twill tape and ribbon from Carolee's Creations.

UNIQUE MEMORY DISPLAYS

Some scrapbook pages are just too pretty to hide away in an album. Here are unique layout ideas that you'll want to keep out where everyone can admire them!

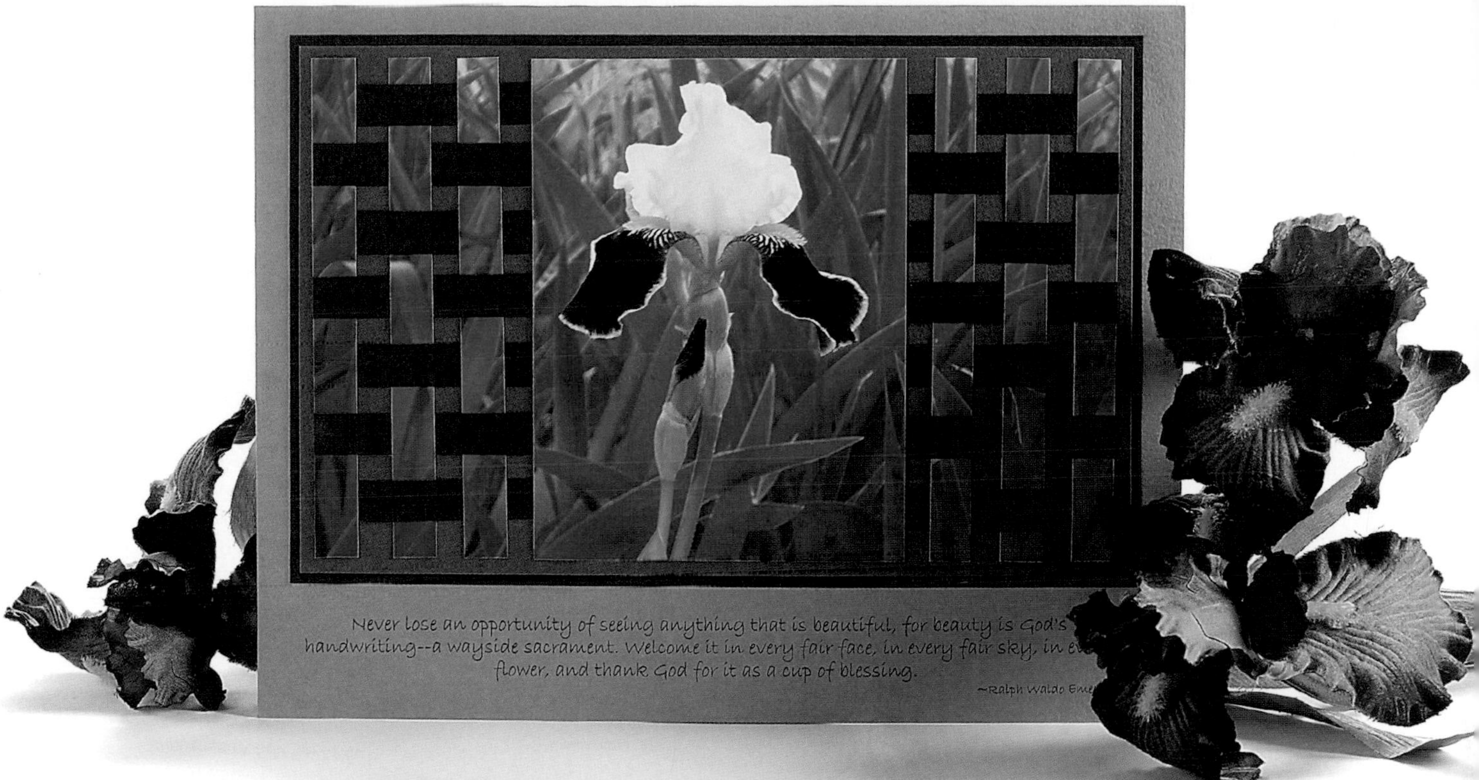

Flower Photo Weave

Design by TAMI MAYBERRY

Strips cut from the main photo are woven into the background colors to create a multicolored mat.

Cut a 10 x 6¼-inch rectangle from purple card stock; cut a 10¼ x 6½-inch rectangle from dark purple card stock. Center and adhere purple card stock to dark purple card stock.

Cut three ½-inch-wide vertical strips from left and right sides of color photo. Center and adhere central portion of photo to purple/dark purple card-stock panel.

Cut 14 (2½ x ½-inch) strips from dark purple card stock. Arrange seven strips horizontally along left edge of photo, spacing strips evenly. Apply glue only to ends of strips adjacent to photo. Repeat on right side of photo with remaining strips of dark purple card stock.

Weave strips cut from sides of photo over and under dark purple card-stock strips, spacing strips evenly. Adhere ends of all strips to purple card stock.

Use computer to generate, or hand-print, this quotation to fit within a 1⅜-inch-tall area across bottom edge of an 11 x 8½-inch piece of green card stock:

Never lose an opportunity of seeing anything that is beautiful, for beauty is God's handwriting—a wayside sacrament. Welcome it in every fair face, in every fair sky, in every flower, and thank God for it as a cup of blessing.

—Ralph Waldo Emerson

Adhere photo panel to green card stock above quotation. ■

SOURCE: Instant-dry paper glue from Beacon.

MATERIALS

- 7½ x 6-inch color photo with main motif contained within center 4½ inches
- Textured card stock: purple, dark purple, green
- Glue runner *or* photo tabs
- Instant-dry paper glue
- Computer with computer fonts (optional)

How does the little busy Bee
Improve each daylight hour,
and gather Honey all day long
from every Blossoming flower!
Intl Flower and Garden Festival
bloom

Busy Bee

Design by SUSAN STRINGFELLOW

Bright colors, a few dimensional embellishments and selective cropping of large photos make for a dynamic memory-book layout.

MATERIALS

- At least 1 digital photo
- Other photos (digital or prints)
- Card stock: 12-inch-square sheet light green; smaller pieces of white, navy blue, light blue, green, purple, lavender
- Striped printed paper
- Photo printing paper
- Card-stock embellishments: alphabet stickers to spell "Bee," round lavender and purple tags
- Purple "bloom" rub-on transfer
- Fibers: white rickrack, green decorative cord
- Complementary buttons: navy blue, light blue, purple, green, lavender
- 5 wire flower clips
- 2 silver eyelets
- Decorative brad
- 1-inch silver safety pin
- Fine sandpaper
- 1-inch-square punch
- ⅛-inch hole punch
- Double-sided adhesive foam squares
- Paper glue
- Computer with computer fonts
- Color computer printer

Project note: *Adhere elements using paper glue unless instructed otherwise.*

Build layout on 12-inch-square sheet of light green card stock. Use computer to generate, or hand-print, verse in upper left corner:

How does the little busy [Bee]
Improve each daylight hour,
And gather Honey all day long
From every Blossoming flower!

Highlight some words by printing them in a larger size and coloring them purple. Leave gap for adding the word "Bee" with stickers.

Sand edges of stickers to spell "Bee"; adhere to layout adjacent to poem.

Print two 6 x 4-inch color copies of the main photo. Cut one into six 2-inch squares; adhere to layout below poem, leaving a scant ¼ inch between squares.

From second photo, crop focal point centered in a 2½-inch square; adhere to white card stock; cut out, leaving narrow border. Adhere to navy blue card stock; cut out, leaving narrow border. Adhere over matching area of photo mosaic with double-sided adhesive foam squares.

Cut a 12 x 3-inch strip of striped printed paper; adhere across layout just below flower mosaic. Adhere white rickrack across top edge of striped printed paper.

Adhere other photos to white card stock; cut out, leaving narrow borders. Adhere photos to upper right and center bottom areas of layout.

Punch 1-inch squares from navy blue, light blue, purple, green and lavender card stock; sand edges. Adhere navy blue square over upper left edge of photo in upper right corner of layout. Arrange remaining squares along bottom of layout, on both sides of photo; adhere.

Adhere a wire flower clip over each card-stock square; adhere matching button to each flower clip.

Print garden information, date, etc., on one round tag; sand edges of that tag and one other. Punch ⅛-inch holes in tags; set silver eyelets in holes. Thread fine green cord through holes; secure cord to rickrack trim near right edge of layout with safety pin and decorative brad.

Adhere blank tag to layout; adhere printed tag with double-sided adhesive foam squares. Transfer "bloom" rub-on to layout across blank tag. ■

SOURCES: Printed papers, stickers, tags, rub-on transfer and buttons from SEI; wire clips and brad from The Paper Studio.

Sunflowers
Like a single sunbeam on a warm day, there is exuberance and brilliance in the sunflower.
Botanical Gardens houston, tx

Sunflower

Design by SUSAN STRINGFELLOW

Print an image on T-shirt transfer paper, then use an iron to transfer the image to burlap for a unique, textural effect.

MATERIALS

- At least 1 digital sunflower photo
- Other sunflower photos (digital or color prints)
- Card stock: 12-inch-square sheets of textured cream, light green
- Printed papers: floral print, solid brown textured
- Green metallic paper
- T-shirt transfer paper
- Printable transparency
- Old paper distress ink
- Yellow acrylic craft paint
- Burlap
- Clear luggage tag
- Gold metal flowers: 1⅜-inch, ⅝-inch
- Tan mini brads
- Beads: square glass floral, metallic E beads
- Iron-on metallic threads
- Complementary fibers, ribbons
- Paintbrush
- Craft knife
- Mini iron
- Glue
- Computer with computer fonts
- Computer printer

Build layout on 12-inch-square sheet of cream textured card stock. Ink edges lightly with old paper distress ink.

Cut a 3¾ x 12-inch piece of floral printed paper; adhere to layout ¾ inch from right edge. Cut a ¼ x 12-inch strip of brown textured paper; adhere to right edge of floral printed paper. Cut three 12-inch lengths of coordinating iron-on metallic threads; fuse threads side by side over seam between floral printed paper and brown paper strip.

Cut a 12 x 2-inch strip green metallic paper; adhere across layout about 1½ inches from bottom edge.

Following manufacturer's instructions, print main photo onto T-shirt transfer paper. Tear edges of the photo while still on the transfer paper. Following manufacturer's instructions, transfer image onto burlap instead of a T-shirt. Trim burlap ½ inch wider all around image.

Near left edge of burlap panel, pull out three vertical threads; replace them with five 7-inch strands of metallic iron-on thread, weaving metallic threads over and under horizontal burlap threads. Trim metallic thread ends even with top edge of burlap; leave excess metallic thread dangling from bottom. Press burlap and metallic threads with iron.

Adhere burlap to upper left corner of layout. Thread beads onto metallic thread ends dangling from bottom of burlap panel.

Adhere remaining three photos to light green card stock; cut out around photos, leaving narrow borders. Arrange photos on layout; adhere.

Use a computer to generate, or hand-print, "Sunflowers" printed in reverse on textured brown paper. Cut out with craft knife; adhere across upper right quadrant of layout.

Attach large gold metal flower to upper right corner of layout with tan mini brad. Attach smaller gold metal flower to lower left corner of burlap photo with tan mini brad.

Cut a 1½-inch square of burlap; cut a 1-inch square of brown textured paper. Lay paper square over burlap square; adhere to lower left corner of layout.

Stamp "Botanical Gardens" or other title onto luggage tag with black ink. Brush yellow acrylic paint across back of luggage tag. Thread three 2-inch lengths of coordinating fiber onto tag; adhere tag to lower left corner of layout, overlapping photo.

Use computer to generate, or hand-print, sunflower quotation onto printable transparency to fit within an area approximately 2 inches square:

Like a single sunbeam on a warm day, there is exuberance and brilliance in the sunflower.

Trim transparency in 2¼-inch square around quotation. Brush yellow acrylic paint across back of transparency to highlight "Sunflower." Adhere upper corners of imprinted transparency to lower left corner of burlap photo with tan mini brads. ■

SOURCES: Printed papers from Diane's Daughters and Provo Craft; metallic paper from Mrs. Grossman's; distress ink from Ranger Industries; metal flowers from Nunn Design; iron-on metallic threads and mini iron from Kreinik.

Imagine

Design by MARY AYRES

Scrapbooking is the perfect way to look back on fond memories. This bright blue collage is the ideal way to honor and inspire a loved one.

MATERIALS

- Photos: 5 x 7-inch color, 1½-inch black-and-white
- 12-inch-square sheets printed card stock: blue squares, graduated blue
- 6 assorted vellum shapes
- 6 assorted acetate word shapes
- Narrow acetate strip with prepunched holes
- Brads: 12 mini black, 4 silver squares
- Silver embellishments: heart hat pin, 1½-inch square frame, heart charm
- 2-inch-wide sheer white ribbon
- Sewing machine with silver metallic thread
- Instant-dry paper glue

Build layout on a 12-inch-square sheet of blue squares printed card stock. Machine-stitch across card stock ¼ inch from top and bottom edges, and again across layout at center of each graduated square on left side; stitch right up to squares, but not through them.

Cut two 5 x 7-inch rectangles from graduated blue printed paper. Arrange rectangles and color photo to right side of layout, overlapping edges; adhere.

Attach an acetate word and vellum shape off-center to each square on the left side of the layout with a square silver brad. Attach an acetate word and vellum shape to bottom of photo using heart charm and silver metallic thread. Attach acetate strip across bottom of layout with 12 black mini brads on left side.

Trim black-and-white photo to fit in frame; adhere photo in frame. Adhere frame to bottom of layout toward left side of page.

Wrap ribbon vertically around layout 1 inch from right edge; tie ends in a bow near top of page. Trim ribbon ends to 3 inches. Attach acetate word and vellum shape to knot with hat pin. ■

SOURCES: Printed card stock, vellum and acetate shapes from AW Cute; silver embellishments from Nunn Design; instant-dry paper glue from Beacon.

grace
dream
live
hope

Lean on Me

Design by SUSAN STRINGFELLOW

Textured paper, torn and folded fabric, dimensional letters and inked edges give a jungle feel to this multilayered memory-book page.

MATERIALS

- Color photos
- Card stock: 12-inch-square sheet green textured, smaller pieces of black
- Printed papers: polka-dot, tropical print, gold
- Decorative foam stamp
- Watermark ink pad
- Spray inks: light green, brown, blue
- Acrylic craft paints, including black
- Fine-tip pen
- 1-inch chipboard letters
- ⅝-inch cork numerals
- Tan self-adhesive mesh
- Muslin fabric
- Fine gold metallic cord
- Shell drops
- Tiny gold heart charm
- Gold mini brads
- Triangle hanger
- Needle
- Paintbrush
- Fine sandpaper
- Glue

Build layout on a 12-inch-square sheet of green textured card stock. Stamp decorative stamp along right side of layout with watermark ink. Lightly brush edges of layout with black acrylic paint.

Cut a 6½ x 9-inch piece of tropical printed paper; sand edges and adhere to upper left corner of layout. Cut a 12 x 1½-inch piece of polka-dot printed paper; sand edges and adhere across layout ¾ inch from bottom edge.

Cut a 6 x 3½-inch piece of mesh; adhere to middle of layout adjacent to right edge.

Adhere main photo to gold printed paper; cut out, leaving a narrow border. Adhere photo to black card stock; cut out, leaving a narrow border.

Thread heart charm and shell drops onto strands of fine gold metallic cord; thread through bottom right edge of photo frame with needle. Knot ends of cord strands. Adhere photo to layout toward upper right corner, 1½ inches from right edge.

Beginning at left edge of second photo, cut three ¼-inch-wide vertical strips, then two ½-inch-wide strips. From right edge, cut three ¼-inch-wide strips. Adhere strips and central portion of photo to gold printed paper in order, leaving ⅛ inch between pieces. Cut out, leaving a ¼-inch border around photo pieces.

Lightly brush edges of gold mat with black acrylic paint; adhere photo to lower left corner of layout.

From muslin fabric tear two ¼ x 2-inch strips and one 1 x 12-inch strip. Spray strips randomly with spray inks.

Accent chipboard letters to spell "LEAN ON ME" with acrylic paints as desired. Tie one of the short fabric strips around the "L." Adhere the chipboard letters to upper left corner of layout. Fold remaining short fabric strip in half; attach to layout below "E" in "ME" with mini brad.

Attach triangle hanger in upper right corner of layout with mini brads. Loop end of longer fabric strip around hanger; secure loop and length of strip to layout with mini brads.

Adhere cork numerals for year over bottom edge of self-adhesive mesh. Add additional date information, journaling, etc., with fine-tip pen. ■

SOURCES: Printed papers from Basic Grey; chipboard letters from Making Memories; cork numerals from LazerLetterz; decorative stamp from Plaid; spray inks from Ranger Industries; shell drops from The Beadery.

LEAN
ON
ME
2005
May
Jeremy and Angie

Time

Design by SANDRA GRAHAM SMITH

This vintage frame will allow time to stand still long enough to admire a loved one's picture.

MATERIALS

- 10 x 8-inch piece of white foam-core board
- Photo
- Card stock: dark brown, medium brown, tan
- Floral striped printed paper
- Rubber stamps: clocks, time-themed words and sayings
- Ink pads: brown, embossing ink
- ⅛-inch gold eyelet
- 1-inch gold clock button
- 6-inch length of gold chain
- ⅛-inch-wide brown ribbon
- Tag punches: 1¾-inch, 2-inch scallop-edged
- ⅛-inch hole punch
- Eyelet-setting tool
- Craft nippers
- Adhesive picture hanger
- Transparent tape
- Double-sided adhesive sheet
- Paper glaze
- Craft cement
- Glue stick

Project note: *Adhere elements using glue stick unless instructed otherwise.*

Lay floral striped printed paper facedown, then place foam-core board on top so that stripes run horizontally; trace around foam-core board onto back of paper and cut out. Adhere floral striped printed paper to foam-core board with double-sided adhesive.

Cut a 5 x 7-inch piece of medium brown card stock. Stamp clock images and time-themed sayings randomly onto card stock with embossing ink. Cut an oval opening in center of stamped card stock; tape photo behind opening.

Stamp a row of small clock and pocket-watch images 7 inches long onto tan card stock with brown ink. Trim top, bottom and left edges straight; trim around curves of clocks along right edge. Adhere strip to left edge of medium brown photo mat.

Adhere photo and mat to dark brown card stock. Trim around edges, leaving a ¼-inch dark brown border.

Stamp "Time" and additional clock images onto tan card stock; cut out. Adhere "Time" to dark brown card stock. Trim around edges, leaving a narrow border; adhere "Time" and remaining stamped images to upper right and lower right corners of photo mat.

Adhere matted photo layout to floral striped printed paper on foam-core board with double-sided adhesive, positioning it toward upper right corner.

Cut a 1 x 10-inch piece of medium brown card stock. Stamp clock images randomly on card stock with embossing ink. Cut a 1½ x 10-inch piece of dark brown card stock. Center and adhere stamped medium brown strip to dark brown strip.

Stamp assorted clock images onto tan card stock with brown ink; cut out. Adhere images to brown card-stock strip. Adhere brown card-stock strip down left side of layout with double-sided adhesive, ¼ inch from edge.

Stamp clock hands onto tan card stock with brown ink; cut out. Adhere clock hands to dark brown card stock; cut out, leaving a narrow border. Punch a ⅛-inch hole through center of clock hands; mount gold eyelet in hole.

Stamp time-themed saying onto tan card stock with brown ink; cut rectangle around words. Adhere rectangle to dark brown card stock; cut out, leaving a narrow dark brown border.

Punch a 2-inch scallop-edged tag from dark brown card stock. Punch a 1⅞-inch tag from floral striped printed paper. Center and adhere floral striped printed paper tag to dark brown card-stock tag; punch ⅛-inch hole in end. Attach one end of chain through hole in tag. Arrange clock hands with eyelet, time-themed saying and tags on bottom of layout as shown; adhere to layout. Cut shank off clock button; adhere to tags with craft cement. Arrange chain; adhere to layout with craft cement.

Apply paper glaze to all stamped clock faces; let dry. Adhere brown ribbon around edges of foam-core board. Center and adhere picture hanger to back. ■

SOURCES: Printed paper from K&Company; rubber stamps from Duncan Enterprises, Stamp Francisco and Great Impressions; punches from EK Success and McGill Inc.; paper glaze from JudiKins.

Time
As every thread of gold is valuable,
so is every minute of time ~ mason

Purr-fect Noel

Design by SUSAN STRINGFELLOW

Pay homage to your favorite feline with this multimedia extravaganza!

MATERIALS

- Digital photo
- 12-inch square watercolor canvas
- Printable canvas
- Tan floral printed paper
- Textured paper: black, green handmade
- Decorative foam stamp
- Acrylic craft paints: white, green
- Rub-on gold metallic finish
- Brown self-adhesive mesh
- "Purr" cat-shaped license plate
- 4½-inch wooden "N"
- Cork flowers
- Brass swirl clip
- Black mini brads
- Small gold heart charm
- Fibers: fine gold metallic cord, ½-inch-wide green ribbon
- Spray preservative
- Paintbrush
- Sewing machine with brown thread
- Craft knife
- Decoupage medium
- Glue
- Dimensional adhesive dots
- Computer with fonts
- Computer printer

Dilute green acrylic paint with a little water; paint canvas with mixture. Dab wet paint with paper towels so that color is uneven. Let dry.

Cut an 11 x 9-inch piece of tan floral printed paper; adhere it to upper left corner of canvas with decoupage medium.

Stamp decorative images in upper right and lower left areas of canvas with white acrylic paint.

Wrap green ribbon around canvas from top to bottom, 2 inches from right edge; adhere ribbon ends on the back.

Cut a 2 x 7½-inch piece of brown mesh; adhere it to upper left corner of canvas ⅝ inch from left edge. Cut a 4-inch square of brown mesh; adhere it to lower right corner of canvas.

Cut a 3 x 4-inch piece of green textured paper; tear the bottom edge and adhere it to lower right corner of layout, over mesh and ribbon, about 1 inch from right edge.

Size main photo to approximately 7¾ x 5½ inches; print onto printable canvas. Size smaller close-up portion of photo to approximately 2½ x 3¼ inches; print onto printable canvas.

Cut out main photo; adhere to black textured paper. Cut out, leaving a narrow border. Rub edges of black paper with gold finish. Machine-stitch around edges of printable canvas with zigzag stitch and brown thread. Adhere photo to upper left corner of canvas, ¾ inch from edges.

Tear smaller photo from printable canvas; adhere to lower right corner of canvas, against right edge. Spray entire canvas with preservative.

Cut a 10-inch piece of green ribbon; tie around wooden "N," attaching brass swirl clip and heart charm in bow. Adhere "N" to bottom of canvas, to left of smaller photo.

Print "oel" reversed on back of black textured paper; cut out with craft knife. Rub surfaces of letters with gold finish; adhere letters next to wooden "N" to complete "Noel."

Stamp cork flowers with foam stamp and white acrylic paint; adhere cork flowers randomly to canvas.

Pierce a hole in each side of "Purr" license plate; thread several 5-inch lengths of gold metallic cord through holes in plate. Adhere plate to lower left side of canvas with dimensional adhesive dots; adhere ends of fibers with black mini brads. ■

SOURCES: Watercolor and printable canvases from Fredrix; printed paper from Jeneva & Co.; license plate from Sticker Studio; cork flowers from LazerLetterz; studs from Scrapworks; brass swirl clip from Making Memories; rub-on gold finish from American Art Clay Co.; spray preservative from Krylon.

PURR
Noel

reminisce
we do not remember days, we remember moments
moments
memories are part of our happiness
days gone by

Easter Moments & Memories

Design by SANDRA GRAHAM SMITH

Remember days gone by in style by displaying an old picture in this unique, bright, pastel pattern that incorporates beautiful fabric ribbon and bottle caps.

Project note: *Adhere elements using pieces cut from double-sided adhesive sheet unless instructed otherwise.*

Center color-block printed paper on foam-core board; trace around foam-core board onto back of paper and cut out.

Photo panel: Cut a 4½ x 5¼-inch piece of green card stock. Cut a 3½ x 4⅞-inch piece of pink card stock. Using pattern provided (page 161), center photo image in oval; trace and cut out. Center and adhere photo to pink card stock.

Adhere "moments" sticker along left edge of green card stock. Adhere pink card stock with photo toward right edge, leaving narrow borders along top, bottom and right edges.

Punch two ⅛-inch holes in upper left corner of green card stock, through end of "moments" sticker. Set eyelets in holes. Wrap ⅛-inch-wide green pin-dot ribbon around upper right and lower right corners of card stock; adhere ends to back. Set photo panel aside.

Adhere two pieces of ⅛-inch-wide green pin-dot ribbon across upper left corner of layout; adhere one piece down center of blue block in lower left corner. Adhere embroidered ribbon across center of layout.

Adhere "reminisce" and "days gone by" stickers to yellow portions of leftover color-block printed paper; cut out, leaving narrow borders. Adhere "reminisce" to upper left and "days gone by" to lower right corner of layout.

Punch seven ⅛-inch holes, evenly spaced, ½ inch to right of green pin-dot ribbon in lower left corner of layout. Punch three ⅛-inch holes ¼ inch to left of "days gone by" sticker. Set eyelets in holes.

Using patterns provided, cut two eggs from leftover color-block printed paper, cutting one from pink area and one from green. Repeat to cut two egg stripes from leftover pink and green areas of color-block printed paper. Center and adhere contrasting stripes to eggs with glue stick; adhere eggs to lower left corner of layout to left of green pin-dot ribbon.

Punch eight flowers from pink card stock; adhere five flowers, evenly spaced, ½–¾ inch to right of eyelets in lower left corner with glue stick.

Using a quarter as a pattern, trace and cut three circles from blue striped portions of leftover color-block printed paper. Center and adhere one of the remaining pink card-stock flowers to each circle with glue stick. Punch a ⅛-inch hole through the center of each; set eyelets in holes. Adhere a circle inside each bottle cap.

Adhere card-stock photo panel to layout 1 inch from top and right edges. Adhere layout to foam-core board. Adhere bottle caps to upper left corner of layout, and to upper right and lower left corners of photo panel. Adhere ⅛-inch-wide green pin-dot ribbon around edges of foam-core board. ■

SOURCES: Printed paper from K&Company; flower punch from Uchida of America.

PATTERNS ON PAGE 161

MATERIALS

- 10 x 8-inch piece of white foam-core board
- Photo
- Card stock: pink, green
- Pastel color-block printed paper
- Word stickers: "moments," "reminisce," "days gone by"
- 15 (⅛-inch) yellow eyelets
- Decorative ribbons: ⅛-inch-wide green-and-white pin-dot, ¼-inch-wide embroidered
- 3 bottle caps
- Small flower punch
- ⅛-inch hole punch
- Eyelet-setting tool
- Double-sided adhesive sheet
- Glue stick

Two

Design by SHERRY WRIGHT

Slim strips of paper tucked into an alphabet-lettered pocket capture every detail of your favorite "terrible two."

MATERIALS

- 7 x 5-inch photo
- Card stock: 8½ x 11-inch sheet of light yellow, 12-inch-square sheet of black
- Word/alphabet printed papers: 12-inch-square sheet of blue-green; tan/multicolored alphabet
- Complementary stickers: alphabet letters to spell "TWO," numeral 2
- Mini book
- Distress ink
- 3 metal key brads
- Label maker with black label tape
- Double-sided adhesive sheet
- Computer with computer fonts (optional)

Build layout on 12-inch-square sheet of blue-green printed paper. Cut two 6-inch squares of tan/multicolored alphabet printed paper. Ink edges of all papers with distress ink.

Adhere one tan/multicolored square to background in upper left corner. Adhere remaining square in lower right corner of layout, forming a pocket by applying adhesive only along side and bottom edges. Adhere photo at an angle across top of layout.

Adhere alphabet stickers to spell "TWO" near upper left corner of layout. Print "TWO" on black label tape with label maker; peel off backing and adhere below alphabet stickers.

Fill mini book with photos and journaling as desired. Ink cover with distress ink; adhere "2" sticker to cover. Adhere mini book to layout to left of photo at angle matching photo.

Use computer to generate, or hand-print, facts about your child in single lines across light yellow card stock. Cut facts apart in narrow strips. Adhere some strips across bottom of layout, staggering their positions as shown. Adhere key brads to left side of layout in spaces between strips. Tuck remaining strips into pocket.

Adhere layout to a 12-inch-square sheet of black card stock. ■

SOURCES: Printed papers and stickers from Scenic Route Paper Co.; mini book from Bazzill; key brads from Making Memories.

TWO
two
2
Wants to eat toast and jelly at every meal
Loves trains, trucks, and helicopters
Knows most of his alphabet
Hair grows very fast and is curly in the back
Says forty words
Screams and claps with delight when he sees Grandma and Grandpa
Likes the LeapFrog alphabet song
Like to play "The Claw" with Dad and be chased around the house

Totally Boy

Design by TAMI MAYBERRY

Full of mischief and spunk, little boys are wonderful inspiration for a scrapbook page.

MATERIALS

- 12 x 12-inch boy-themed card stock with matching 12 x 12-inch vellum
- Alphabet foam stamps
- Date stamp
- Light blue twill tape
- White acrylic paint
- White alphabet rub-on transfers
- Coordinating stickers
- Clear acrylic stickers
- Desired photos
- Sandpaper
- Paintbrush
- Sponge brush
- Sewing machine with white all-purpose thread
- Paper adhesive

Adhere a 5 x 7-inch photo on the left side of a sheet of card stock. Position a 12 x 12-inch sheet of matching vellum on top of card stock; machine-stitch along left edge and along white lines in pattern on vellum. Attach adhesive dots in upper and lower right corners to secure.

Carefully tear a small hole in the vellum over the center of photo; begin to peel back the vellum until desired portion of photo is exposed. Tear edges and roll under to secure.

Lay a piece of twill tape along left edge of vellum; wrap ends to back and secure with double-sided tape. Use sponge brush to apply white paint to foam stamps to stamp desired name underneath photo opening; let dry.

Use a stiff brush to lightly paint over the "boy" title on right side of vellum. Paint a small strip of white paint in bottom right corner of page. Apply white paint to date stamp and ink desired year in lower left corner on twill tape. Let paint dry.

Carefully tear and peel back a small piece of vellum in the corner underneath photo opening; lightly sand a sticker and attach it in torn area. Top sticker with a clear acrylic sticker.

Tear a small hole in "boy" title area on right side of vellum; fold back edges. Transfer "all" onto top portion of vellum that was folded back. Lightly sand exposed card stock.

Lightly sand desired sticker; attach in upper right corner, hiding adhesive dot. Attach an acrylic sticker in lower right corner on top of paint strip to hide adhesive dot. ■

SOURCES: Card stock, vellum and stickers from American Crafts; twill tape from Creek Bank Creations; foam stamps and rub-on transfers from Making Memories; acrylic stickers from Creative Imaginations.

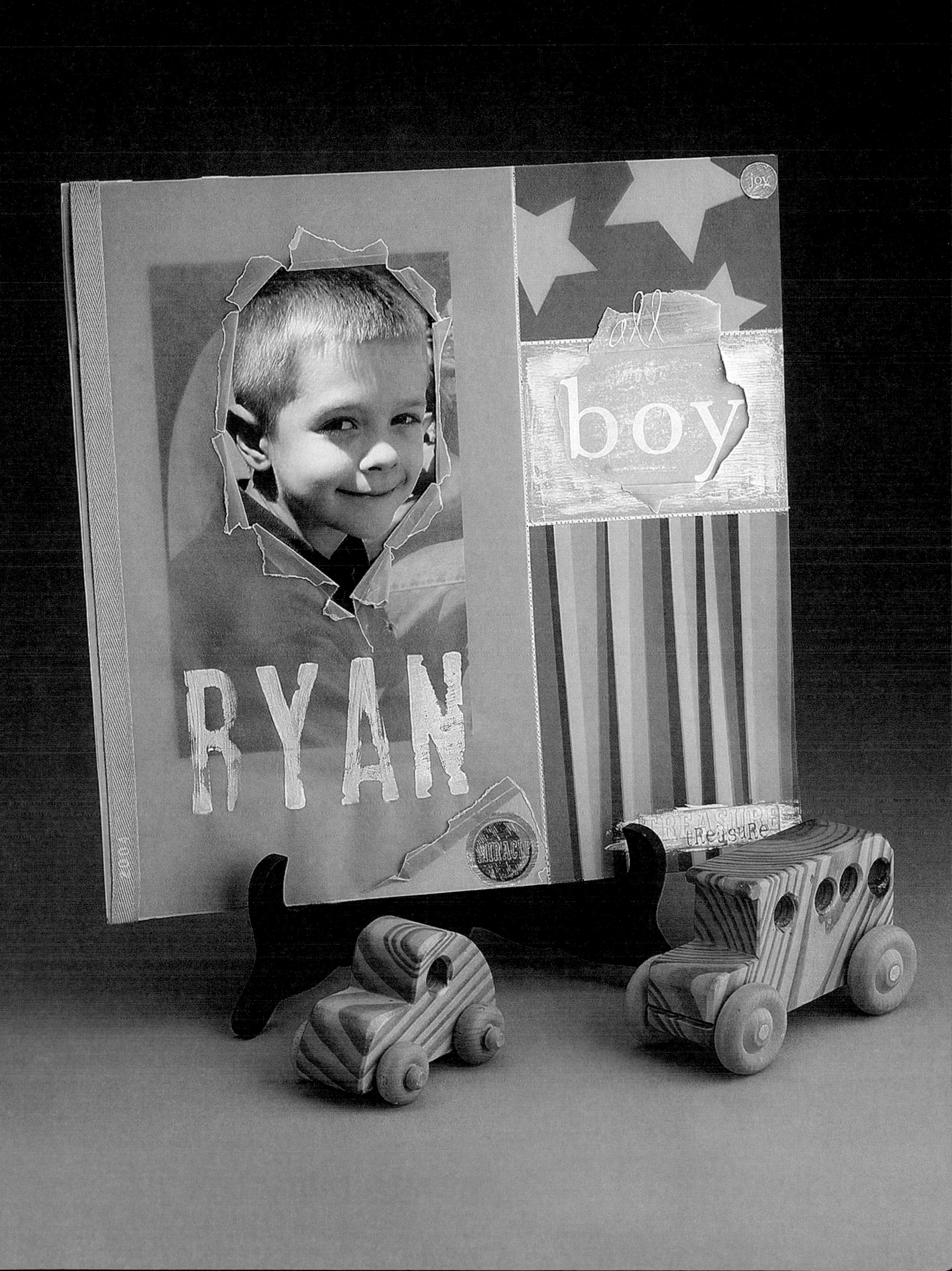
joy
all
boy
RYAN
TREASURE
treasure

Cheyenne Rose

Design by MARY AYRES

Frame a portrait of a special girl with bottle caps, metal brads, tie-ons and lots of pink!

MATERIALS

- 4¾ x 6¾-inch color photo
- 12-inch-square sheet pink block printed paper
- Card stock: medium pink, dark pink, lime green, white
- Card-stock shapes: pink, red
- Assorted vellum shapes
- Assorted acetate word shapes
- Brads: mini silver, mini black, mini pink, mini flower, silver heart, silver star
- Silver embellishments: 1-inch silver flower, 1¾-inch oval bookplate, flower paper clip, buckle, tag
- Additional embellishments: pink bottle cap, buttons, alphabet charms, key charm, metal-rim square tag, "happy" acrylic tile, crystal flower
- Fibers: green craft thread, silver metallic craft thread, pink ribbons
- Needle
- Hole punch
- Instant-dry paper glue
- Computer with computer fonts (optional)

Adhere 12-inch-square sheet of pink block printed paper to 12-inch square of white card stock; set aside.

Cut a 5¾ x 7¾-inch rectangle from medium pink card stock, a 5¼ x 7¼-inch rectangle from lime green card stock, and a 5 x 7-inch rectangle from dark pink card stock. Center and adhere rectangles to each other; center and adhere photo to top rectangle.

Use computer to generate, or hand-print, name—except for first initial—on white card stock. Trim rectangle around name, leaving room for alphabet charm at beginning. Adhere white card stock to medium pink card stock. Cut out, leaving narrow border.

Stitch alphabet charm to name rectangle with green craft thread. Attach name label to right side of photo rectangle with silver flower paper clip. Center and adhere photo rectangle to layout.

Embellish blocks around photo layout with a mixture of card stock, vellum and acetate shapes and other embellishments. ■

SOURCES: Printed paper, card stock, vellum and acetate shapes from AW Cute; instant-dry paper glue from Beacon.

encourage
play
Fun
grow
Cheyenne Rose
HAPPY
Laughter
Create

All Boy

Design by SHERRY WRIGHT

A denim pocket snipped from a worn pair of jeans anchors the color palette of this boy-themed layout.

Build layout on 12-inch-square sheet of solid black paper. Cut a 12 x 6-inch piece of circles printed paper; adhere across center of layout. Cut a 4 x 12-inch piece of blue solid paper; adhere along left side of layout, near edge. Cut a 6 x 5½-inch piece of bars printed paper; adhere to bottom left corner of layout. Cut a 6 x 6½-inch piece of bars printed paper; adhere at an angle to upper right corner of layout.

Machine-stitch blue jeans pocket to lower right corner of layout with white thread and zigzag stitch. In same manner, machine-stitch over right edge of blue solid paper panel on left side of layout.

Stamp "ALL" in upper left corner with foam stamps and black pigment ink.

Spray "B," "O" and "Y" chipboard stencils and chipboard frame with blue ink. When dry, sand edges of all pieces.

Adhere outer portion of "B" stencil to blue solid paper under "ALL"; adhere letters punched from "O" and "Y" stencils beside "B." Adhere "B" punched from "B" stencil (or stencil initial for child's name) to denim pocket.

Trim a piece of circles printed paper to fit behind chipboard frame. Apply rub-on transfers to read "100%" to center of printed paper. Adhere paper behind frame; adhere frame to layout to right of "ALL."

Adhere 5 x 7-inch photo to upper left corner of layout at an angle; adhere 4 x 5-inch photo to lower left corner of layout. Adhere bottle cap over lower left corner of larger photo.

Print child's name and phrases—"unique," "tough," "cool," etc.—on black label tape with label maker. Peel off backing; adhere to layout as desired.

Cut ½ x 3-inch strips from printed papers. Write facts and journaling on strips; tuck strips into denim pocket. ■

SOURCES: Printed papers from Basic Grey; stencils and foam stamps from Making Memories; chipboard frame and bottle cap from Li'l Davis Designs; spray ink from Ranger Industries; rub-on transfers from Autumn Leaves.

MATERIALS

- Photos: 5 x 7 inches, 4 x 5 inches
- Printed papers: 12-inch-square sheet of solid black; bars and circles prints in shades of blue, gold, white and gray; and complementary blue solid
- Chipboard accents: stencils to spell "BOY," 3¼ x 1½-inch frame
- Foam stamps: alphabet, numerals
- Ink: blue spray, black pigment
- Black rub-on transfers: numerals, percent sign
- Patch pocket cut from blue jeans
- "Adventure" bottle cap
- Label maker with black label tape
- Sewing machine with white thread
- Fine sandpaper
- Double-sided adhesive sheet

Families

Design by MARY AYRES

An antique brass drawer pull tops this shadow-box frame filled with vintage family photos.

MATERIALS
- 14¼-inch-square wooden memory frame
- 8 small photos
- Card stock: white, neutral
- 12-inch square of yellow distressed-wood printed paper
- Plain vellum
- Off-white mulberry paper
- Postcard rubber stamp
- Ink pads: brown, black
- Brown acrylic craft paint
- Fabric roman-shade frame
- Assorted pearl buttons
- Gold heart charm
- ⅛-inch gold eyelets
- Metal drawer pull
- Antique lace
- Decorative off-white cord
- Paintbrush
- Fine sandpaper
- Small dry sponge
- ⅛-inch hole punch
- Eyelet-setting tool
- Instant-dry paper glue
- Double-sided adhesive foam squares
- Computer with computer fonts (optional)

Project note: *Adhere elements with instant-dry paper glue unless instructed otherwise.*

Paint frame with brown acrylic paint. Sand surfaces and edges to give it a distressed look.

Ink edges of printed paper with dry sponge and brown ink pad. Center and adhere distressed-wood printed paper inside frame. Adhere decorative cord around edges of distressed-wood printed paper, butting ends together in corner.

Adhere photos to plain vellum. Tear vellum around photos ¼ inch from edge. Ink torn edges with brown ink.

Plan placement of photos. Punch two ⅛-inch holes in each photo; set eyelets in holes. Thread decorative cord loosely in and out of eyelets; adhere cord ends to back of one photo. Adhere photos to distressed-wood printed paper in frame with double-sided adhesive foam squares.

Use computer to generate, or hand-print, "families are tied together with heart strings" on plain vellum to fit within an area measuring approximately 3¼ x 1¼ inches. Stamp postcard image onto white card stock with black ink.

Trim printed vellum and stamped image to fit behind fabric frame. Adhere edges of fabric frame to mulberry paper; tear mulberry paper around edges of fabric frame. Adhere lace to back of mulberry paper.

Center and adhere entire piece to distressed-wood printed paper in frame with double-sided adhesive foam squares.

String heart charm onto decorative cord; loop cord around ribbon on fabric frame. Adhere buttons to central motif and photos as desired.

Cut four 7⅛ x 1-inch strips from white card stock and four from neutral card stock. Randomly stamp postcard images all over strips with black ink. ***Note:*** *To achieve the softer look shown, stamp first onto scrap paper and then onto card stock.* Miter one corner of each white strip, cutting two in one direction and two in the opposite direction. Repeat with neutral strips. Ink edges of strips with brown ink.

Arrange card-stock strips on frame, alternating colors, with mitered edges meeting neatly in the corners. Adhere strips to frame.

Center and adhere drawer pull at top of frame. ■

SOURCES: Frame from Walnut Hollow; printed paper from K&Company; postcard stamp from Plaid/All Night Media; fabric roman-shade frame from EK Success; instant-dry paper glue from Beacon.

families are tied together
with heart strings

tHe ManY ColoRs
Of
LUCAS

The Many Colors of Lucas

Design by BARBARA GREVE

Bright blocks of color behind see-through plastic letters hint at a loved one's multilayered personality.

Print four full-size copies of photo onto white inkjet paper with photo-editing software, tinting one photo blue, one red, one green and one yellow.

Cut 12 x 2½-inch strips from color-block printed papers as follows: two strips from citrus, two from light green, one from raspberry. Adhere strips vertically to 12-inch-square sheet of plain white paper, positioning raspberry strip in center. Trim edges even with edges of white paper.

Cut tinted photos into 2½-inch squares. Cut several 2½-inch squares from each sheet of printed paper. Arrange and adhere photo squares on 12-inch-square panel in mosaic fashion, centering photo and positioning bottom edge 3¾ inches from bottom of 12-inch-square panel. Adhere squares cut from printed papers as desired.

Punch ⅛-inch hole in each outer corner of acrylic frame and at top center of each acrylic letter. Lightly mark position of acrylic frame on layout; apply embroidery stitch rub-on transfers to layout where edges of frame will be.

Arrange acrylic frame and letters to spell name on layout; mark positions of holes and pierce all layers with paper piercer. Attach frame and letters to layout with mini brads.

Print small color copy of photo onto photo paper; trim to fit in 1-inch frame. Mount photo in frame. Tie 1-inch frame around bottom of acrylic frame with orange net ribbon. Knot organdy ribbon around bottom of "S."

Apply alphabet rub-on transfers to layout to spell "the many colors of." ■

SOURCES: Printed papers and organdy ribbon from Doodlebug Design Inc.; rub-on transfers from K&Company and KI Memories; acrylic alphabet and frame from Heidi Swapp/Advantus Corp.; metal frame from K&Company; fabric adhesive from Beacon; photo-editing effects from www.picasa.com.

MATERIALS

- Digital photo
- White inkjet paper
- White photo paper
- 12-inch-square sheet of plain white paper
- 12-inch-square sheets of color-block printed papers: raspberry, light green, citrus
- Rub-on transfers: embroidery stitches in assorted colors; assorted alphabet letters in red, light blue, dark blue, light green
- Clear acrylic page accents: 5 x 6-inch frame, 2-inch alphabet letters
- 1-inch-square plastic frame
- Mini brads in assorted bright colors
- Fibers: ¼-inch-wide orange net ribbon, ½-inch-wide sheer turquoise organdy polka-dot ribbon
- ⅛-inch hole punch
- Paper piercer
- Permanent adhesive
- Computer with photo-editing software
- Computer printer

One With Nature

Design by SUSAN HUBER

Echo the design elements of a photo in a scrapbook layout using torn paper, fiber, tags and ink.

MATERIALS

- 2 copies of color photo
- Card stock: 12-inch-square sheet of dark green; pieces of tan, brown, assorted greens
- Self-adhesive vellum in seasonal colors
- 3 manila tags
- Blow pens
- Fine-tip pens for slick surfaces
- Chalks
- Sugar beads
- Gold mini brads
- Fine twine: natural-color, dark green
- Foam tape
- Double-sided tape
- Computer with computer fonts (optional)

Build layout on a 12-inch-square sheet of dark green card stock. Tear pieces from tan and brown card stocks; overlap them on bottom portion of layout; adhere along bottom edge.

Tear additional pieces of assorted green card stocks for rocks; adhere to brown and tan layers.

Using several complementary colors of blow pens and chalks, color brown layers to give the appearance of an outdoor setting.

Tear ½-inch-wide strips from three different green card stocks. Adhere long pieces up sides of layout for tree trunks. Tear shorter pieces; adhere for branches.

Tear strips of self-adhesive vellum for sun's rays; adhere strips to layout radiating down and out from the top center edge.

Adhere strands of natural-color twine along sun's rays. Wrap ends over top of layout; adhere on back.

Adhere one photo to dark green card stock; tear along bottom edge and cut along side and top edges, leaving a narrow border. Adhere photo panel to light green card stock; tear along bottom edge and cut along side and top edges, leaving a narrow border. Add details to light green border with dark green fine-tip pen.

Tear second copy of photo around edges. Adhere photo to tan card stock; tear edges and color with chalk. Coat surface of torn photo with smooth strips of double-sided tape. Remove second backing strip; dip photo, sticky side down, into sugar beads. Press beads into place. Repeat as needed until image is coated with sugar beads.

Adhere beaded image to dark green card stock; tear around edges. Adhere matted image to tan card stock; tear around edges. Add dots randomly to torn edges of card stock with fine-tip pens. Adhere beaded image to layout over main photo's lower right corner.

Use computer to generate, or hand-print, letter outlines of words "ONE," "WITH" and "NATURE" on manila tags. Add dots and lines along edges of tags with fine-tip pens. Tear ends off tags; chalk all edges.

Tie dark green twine bows through holes in tags. Adhere tags to layout below photos with foam tape. ■

SOURCES: Vellum from Emagination Crafts; sugar beads from PennyWise Arts; blow pens from Color Workshop; fine-tip pens from American Crafts.

ONE
WITH
NATURE

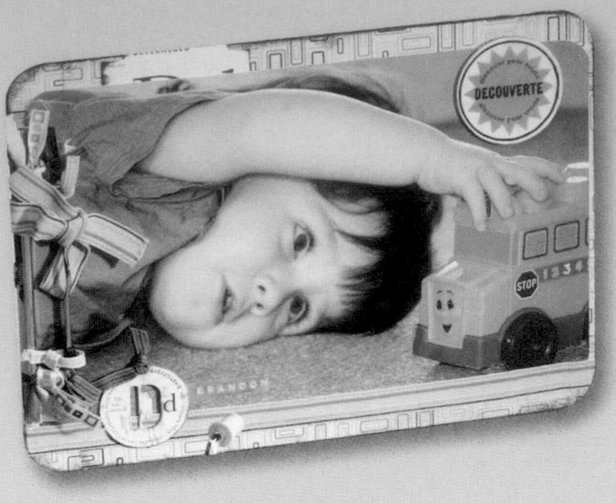

FRAMES

Wrap favorite photos in custom-created frames that enhance and display them to the best advantage.

Retro Drive-in Frame

Design by SUSAN STRINGFELLOW

Pull on your poodle skirt and saddle shoes—one look at this frame will have you bebopping down memory lane!

MATERIALS

- 10 x 8-inch frame
- 2 photos
- Black card stock
- Printed paper: light green-and-white retro starburst, red-and-white striped, multicolored striped
- Vintage card-stock cutouts with alphabet
- 2½-inch image of model rocket
- Distress inks: pale brown, ivory
- 3 rhinestone brads
- Light green triangle clip
- ⅝-inch-wide white satin ribbon
- Fine sandpaper
- ⅛-inch hole punch
- Sewing machine with white thread
- Eyelet-setting tool
- Craft knife
- Spray preservative
- Matte decoupage medium
- Adhesive foam squares
- Spray adhesive

Project note: *Use matte decoupage medium for adhesive unless instructed otherwise.*

Measure and cut light green printed paper to fit on front of frame; adhere paper to frame. Sand edges with sandpaper; ink with ivory distress ink.

Cut a 9 x ½-inch strip of red-and-white striped printed paper with stripes running lengthwise. Machine-stitch down center of strip with a straight stitch. Ink edges with pale brown distress ink; adhere strip up left side of frame.

Cut a 10 x 1¼-inch strip of multicolored striped printed paper with stripes running across short width. Machine-stitch ¼ inch from each long edge with a zigzag stitch. Ink edges with pale brown distress ink; center and adhere strip across bottom of frame.

Trim accent photo to fit in lower right corner of frame. Sand edges. Adhere photo to frame; adhere triangle clip over edge of photo.

Cut a 2-inch square of red-and-white striped printed paper; adhere vintage label to square at an angle. Ink edges with pale brown distress ink. Cut and fold ribbon into a small tab; affix to top of printed paper square with rhinestone brad. Adhere square to upper right corner of frame with adhesive foam squares.

Ink edges of another vintage label with pale brown distress ink. Cut and fold ribbon into a small tab; affix to right edge of label with rhinestone brad. Adhere label to lower left corner of frame.

Ink edges of another vintage label with pale brown distress ink. Cut and fold ribbon into a small bow; affix to left edge of label with rhinestone brad. Adhere label to left side of frame with adhesive foam squares.

Trim another label to fit on frame near upper left corner; ink edges with ivory distress ink and adhere to frame.

Cut out model rocket image with craft knife; adhere to left side of frame, overlapping top label.

Cut individual letters from card-stock label sheet to spell "Drive In"; cut out in irregular shapes. Adhere cutout letters to black card stock; cut out, leaving narrow, uneven borders. Ink letters with ivory distress ink; adhere letters across bottom of frame. ■

SOURCES: Frame, printed papers and vintage card-stock label sheet from Heart & Home Inc./Melissa Frances; rhinestone brads from SEI; distress inks from Ranger Industries; triangle clip from Altered Pages; matte decoupage medium from Golden Artist Colors; preservative spray and adhesive from Krylon.

Here's Looking at You, Kid

Design by SANDRA GRAHAM SMITH

This frightening festive frame is a great way to capture the younger years of trick-or-treating.

MATERIALS

- Acrylic double frame for 3½ x 5-inch photos
- Photo
- Halloween-themed printed papers: polka-dot, striped, phrases
- Candy-corn goody-bag sticker
- Glue stick

Cut a 3½ x 5-inch piece of Halloween phrases printed paper. Using pattern provided (page 161), cut four corners from striped printed paper; adhere to corners of phrases printed paper.

Using pattern provided, trim photo in an oval to fit on phrases printed paper background; adhere, positioning photo toward top of background.

Cut "Halloween" from phrases printed paper, leaving a dot at each end. Adhere phrase to orange portion of striped printed paper; trim, leaving a narrow orange border. Adhere phrase at an angle across bottom of photo layout.

Cut a 3½ x 5-inch piece of striped printed paper and a 2 x 3-inch piece of polka-dot printed paper. Center and adhere polka-dot printed paper to striped printed paper. Adhere candy-corn goody-bag sticker at an angle to polka-dot printed paper.

Cut "Cute Costumes!" and "Trick or Treat" from phrases printed paper, leaving a dot at each end of each phrase. Adhere phrases at angles across top and bottom of striped printed paper.

Cut two 3½ x 5-inch pieces of striped printed paper; adhere one to the back of the photo panel and the other to the back of the goody-bag sticker panel. Slide layouts into frame.■

SOURCES: Printed papers from Creative Imaginations; sticker from Colorbök.

PATTERNS ON PAGE 161

Dance Recital

Design by SANDRA GRAHAM SMITH

A tiny invitation peeks from an envelope glued to the front of a purchased plastic frame, while layers of torn paper surround an oval mat.

Cut a 3½ x 4½-inch piece of black card stock. Cut oval in upper right corner for photo.

Tear two 1¾-inch-wide strips of musical score printed paper. Adhere one to left edge of black card stock and the second to right edge. Trim printed paper even with outer edges of black card stock and oval opening.

Tear a 1-inch-wide strip of musical notes printed paper. Adhere down left edge of layout, over musical score printed paper. Trim edges even with edges of layout.

Tape photo behind oval opening. Cut a 3½ x 4½-inch piece of musical notes printed paper; adhere to back of layout. Insert entire layout into acrylic frame.

Invitation: Cut a 1 x 1½-inch piece of musical score printed paper. Adhere to black card stock; trim, leaving a narrow black border.

Use computer to generate, or hand-print, "Dance Recital Today!" or other message on plain white paper to fit within rectangle measuring 13/16 x 3/8 inch; cut out. Adhere message at top of invitation; insert in open envelope.

Trim treble clef from musical notes printed paper; adhere to envelope. Adhere envelope with invitation to lower right corner of acrylic frame. ■

SOURCES: Printed papers from Provo Craft and Design Originals.

MATERIALS

- 3½ x 4½-inch acrylic frame
- Photo
- Black card stock
- Music-themed printed paper: musical score, musical notes
- Plain white paper
- 1½ x 1-inch plain white paper envelope
- Glue stick
- Double-sided adhesive sheet
- Computer with computer font (optional)

DETERMINED
discover your world
DECOUVERTE
discover your world
STOP
1234
BRANDON
determined
NINE
6
EIGHT
8
T
P
E
O
C

Playtime

Design by SHERRY WRIGHT

A clipboard embellished with ribbons and die cuts makes a fantastic base for a treasured hand-tinted photograph.

Project note: *Adhere elements using pieces cut from a double-sided adhesive sheet unless instructed otherwise.*

Cut printed paper to cover front of clipboard, piecing together strips at clip end. Adhere multicolored printed paper to clipboard, applying decoupage medium to clipboard and to back of multicolored printed paper pieces with a foam brush. Smooth out wrinkles with your finger. Let dry, then trim excess paper along edges.

Round off corners of photo to mimic curved corners of clipboard. With clipboard clip on the left, adhere photo to center of clipboard. Adhere wider ribbon across clipboard over bottom edge of photo; adhere ribbon ends on back of clipboard.

Cut 8-inch pieces from assorted ribbons; knot around clipboard clip. Cut a 24-inch piece of wider ribbon; tie in a bow around center of clip.

Ink edges of card-stock tab with distress ink; adhere to upper left corner of clipboard, tucking end behind photo. Adhere chipboard coaster over photo in upper right corner.

Ink edges of card-stock round tag with distress ink; knot ribbon through hole in tag. Adhere tag over photo and ribbon in lower left corner. Print out name on gold label tape; adhere to photo in lower left corner, tucking end behind card-stock tag.

Hanger: Tie loop in center of a 28-inch piece of ribbon; adhere ribbon ends to back of clipboard. Tie coordinating ribbon in a bow around loop of first ribbon. ■

SOURCES: Printed paper and coordinating ribbons from KI Memories; chipboard coaster from Li'l Davis Designs; card-stock tab and round tag from Autumn Leaves; decoupage medium from Plaid.

MATERIALS

- 12½ x 9-inch clipboard
- 12 x 8-inch photo
- Multicolored printed paper
- Chipboard coaster
- "D for determined" card-stock round tag and tab
- Distress ink
- Yellow paper clip
- Decorative ribbons
- Foam brush
- Corner rounder punch
- Label maker with gold label tape
- Double-sided adhesive sheet
- Decoupage medium

Mini Bouquet Frame

Design by SHERRY WRIGHT

What a perfect way to display this hand-tinted photo! Using foam tape gives this mini bouquet the dimensional effect it needs to show off your loved one's picture.

MATERIALS

- Photo
- Card stock: pink, light green
- Pastel harlequin printed paper
- Chipboard
- Bouquet rubber stamp
- Ink pads: pastel blue, rose pink
- Colored pencils
- 18 inches ⅜-inch-wide green-and-white gingham checked ribbon
- Self-adhesive magnet strips
- Corner rounder punch
- Die-cutter with large frame die (optional)
- Double-sided adhesive sheet
- Foam tape

Cut 4½-inch strip of harlequin printed paper and another of chipboard. Cut a large frame from each with die-cutter. ***Option:*** *Use ruler and craft knife to cut 4 x 4⅞-inch frames from harlequin printed paper and chipboard.* Adhere harlequin printed paper frame to front of chipboard frame with double-sided adhesive.

Cut a 3⅞ x 4⅞-inch piece of pink card stock; adhere to back of frame along sides and bottom with double-sided adhesive, leaving top edge open for inserting photo.

Stamp bouquet image on light green card stock with pastel blue ink; trim 1½ x 2-inch rectangle around image. Round off corners with corner punch. Color stamped image with colored pencils; ink edges of card stock with rose pink ink pad. Adhere stamped image to upper left corner of frame with foam tape.

Wrap ribbon around bottom of frame, tying ends in a bow in lower right corner.

Adhere two 2¾-inch-long magnet strips to back of frame. ■

SOURCES: Printed papers from Paper Salon; die-cutting system and large frame die from Sizzix/Ellison.

Cut a piece of chipboard 10 x 8 inches. Cut birch trees printed paper to fit on chipboard; adhere. Ink edges of chipboard with silver leafing pen.

Cut four 6½ x 1-inch strips of textured dark blue card stock. Stamp strips with floral background image and watermark ink. Sprinkle a generous amount of silver mica powder onto wet ink; brush off excess with paintbrush.

Trim one short end of each strip with decorative-edge scissors; trim other short ends at an angle—two in one direction, two in the other, so that ends will meet as mitered corners. Ink edges of strips with silver leafing pen.

Arrange strips in upper left and lower right corners of chipboard like a frame, leaving a narrow space around edges and between diagonal edges in corners; adhere.

Cut canvas-texture photo card in half, reserving one piece for another use. Print photo on remaining portion of card; trim to 6 x 4 inches with decorative-edge scissors. Ink edges with silver leafing pen.

Adhere photo to cork sheet; trim around edges with regular scissors, leaving a narrow border. Adhere photo to frame.

Adhere fishnet to chipboard, overlapping photo, applying craft cement to knots of net.

"Shore" letter tiles: Cut five 1½ x 2-inch pieces of chipboard. Stamp letters to spell "SHORE" on birch trees printed paper with foam alphabet stamps and dark blue pigment ink, leaving room around letters to cut out. Sprinkle embossing powder onto wet ink; emboss. Cut out letters to fit on chipboard tiles; adhere. Chalk tiles with brown chalk; ink edges and very narrow border around front with silver leafing pen. Adhere tiles across bottom of frame.

"At the" tag: Cut one 3 x ½-inch piece of chipboard. Stamp letters to spell "AT THE" on birch trees printed paper to fit tag with ¾-inch alphabet stamps and dark blue pigment ink. Cut out words, leaving room at left end for eyelet; adhere to tag. Chalk tag with brown chalk; ink edges and very narrow border around front with silver leafing pen.

Punch a ⅛-inch hole in left end of tag; set eyelet in hole. Thread jute through eyelet; knot; trim and fray jute ends. Adhere tag to frame, overlapping photo.

Charms: Remove split rings from round metal-rim tags. Punch three 1⅛-inch circles from cork sheet; center and adhere one to each tag. Punch ⅛-inch circle through each tag; reattach split rings.

Attach a charm to each tag, hanging jump ring from split ring. Adhere charm to cork with craft cement. Thread split rings of tags onto net; adhere tags with craft cement.

Fill glass bottle with sand; attach to net with jump ring in stopper.

Hanger: Attach D-rings at top corners of frame with silver brads. Tie cord ends to D-rings. ■

SOURCES: Canvas photo card from Strathmore; printed paper from Paper House Productions; alphabet stamps from Making Memories and Authentic Models Inc.; floral stamp from Stampington & Co.; glass bottle from 7gypsies; watermark ink from Tsukineko; mica powder from Jacquard Products.

MATERIALS

- Chipboard
- Digital photo
- Dark blue textured card stock
- Birch trees printed paper
- Canvas-texture computer photo-printing card
- 3 (1¼-inch) round metal-rim tags with split rings
- Rubber stamps: floral background pattern, ¾-inch alphabet
- 1½-inch stencil-style alphabet foam stamps
- Ink pads: watermark ink, dark blue pigment ink
- Silver mica powder
- Clear embossing powder
- Brown chalk
- Silver leafing pen
- Cork sheet
- 10 x 8-inch section fishnet
- 3 silver nautical charms
- 1-inch glass bottle with stopper
- Sand
- 2 silver D-rings picture-hanging hardware
- 2 silver brads
- ⅛-inch silver eyelet
- Silver jump rings
- Jute twine
- Beige cord
- Small paintbrush
- 1⅛-inch circle punch
- ⅛-inch hole punch
- Decorative-edge scissors
- Eyelet-setting tool
- Embossing heat tool
- Paper glue
- Craft cement
- Computer with printer

Beach Frame

Design by SUSAN HUBER

Add 3-D texture to your next project with colored embossing powders and melted "chips."

STAMPED TILES

Place lid on mini electric frying pan; preheat pan to HIGH. Lay nonstick crafting sheet in hot pan.

Lay chipboard tile on crafting sheet. Sprinkle tile with clear, deep-impression embossing powder to cover. As clear embossing powder melts, sprinkle tile with pinches of both blue embossing powders, allowing colors to blend.

When embossing powder is completely melted, remove tile from skillet. Press a fish rubber stamp into the melted embossing powder. Allow tile to cool, then lift off rubber stamp.

Repeat to make a total of 14 blue tiles, using a variety of fish rubber stamps.

In the same manner, make a total of 10 gold tiles, sprinkling melting deep-impression embossing powder with pinches of both gold embossing powders, and stamping tiles with a variety of seashell rubber stamps.

When tiles are completely cool, ink edges of blue tiles with silver leafing pen and edges of gold tiles with gold leafing pen.

ASSEMBLY

Cut a 9½ x 11¼-inch piece of dark blue card stock. Cut an 8⅞ x 10⅝-inch piece of yellow card stock. Center and adhere yellow card stock to dark blue card stock; set aside.

Cut an 8½ x 6⅞-inch piece of medium blue card stock; cut a 4⅞ x 3-inch opening in center. Ink edges of center opening with silver leafing pen.

Referring to photo throughout, arrange blue tiles on blue card stock; adhere with double-sided tape. Adhere photo behind opening in frame.

Cut an 8½ x 3½-inch piece of yellow card stock. Arrange gold tiles on yellow card stock; adhere with double-sided tape.

Adhere medium blue and yellow panels with photo and tiles to layers of dark blue and yellow textured card stock created earlier, referring to photo for placement.

Adhere easel to back of frame. Wrap fibers around frame where blue and yellow panels meet; knot ends off to the left; suspend silver crab charm from knot. ■

SOURCES: Seashell stamps from Hero Arts; deep-impression embossing powder from Mark Industries; leafing pens from Krylon.

MATERIALS

- 4¾ x 3-inch photo
- Card stock: dark blue, medium blue, yellow
- 24 (1½-inch-square) chipboard tiles
- Rubber stamps: assorted fish, seashells
- Clear deep-impression embossing powder
- Regular embossing powders: blue, light blue, gold, light gold
- Metallic leafing pens: gold, silver
- Decorative fibers
- Silver crab charm
- Adhesive-backed cardboard frame easel
- Heat embossing tool
- Nonstick crafting sheet
- Miniature electric frying pan
- Double-sided tape

Beautiful Blossoms Frame

MATERIALS

- 7¼ x 5¾-inch flat frame with 4½ x 3-inch opening
- Photo
- Pink/brown/white/green floral printed paper
- Plain white paper
- Flower-box rubber stamp
- Brown ink pad
- Colored pencils
- Pink acrylic craft paint
- Cream silk flower petals
- 3 gold mini brads
- Pink rickrack
- Paintbrush
- Foam brush
- Fine sandpaper
- Decoupage medium
- Foam tape
- Double-sided adhesive sheet

Design by SHERRY WRIGHT

Silk flowers, pink rickrack and retro blossoms embellish a fun and funky frame.

Paint side edges and back of frame pink; let dry.

Cut four 5½ x 1⅜-inch strips from floral printed paper; ink edges with brown ink pad.

Apply decoupage medium to front of frame and back of floral printed paper strips with foam brush. Adhere floral printed paper strips to front of frame, first across top and bottom, and then up sides. Smooth out wrinkles with your fingers. Let dry.

Trim excess paper. Sand edges of frame with sandpaper. Adhere rickrack across bottom of frame with decoupage medium.

Stamp flower-box image on plain white paper with brown ink; trim rectangle around image. Color stamped image with colored pencils; ink edges of rectangle with brown ink pad. Adhere rectangle to lower right corner of frame with foam tape.

Brush mini brads with pink acrylic paint; let dry. Sand mini brads lightly. Poke mini brads through silk flower petals; adhere flower petals in upper left corner of frame. ■

SOURCES: Frame from EK Success; printed papers, rubber stamp and ink from Paper Salon; decoupage medium from Plaid.

Authentic Girl

Design by KATHLEEN PANEITZ

Sanded paper edges and fabric accents make this frame, hung from a polka-dot ribbon and silver clips, shout "100 percent girl!"

MATERIALS

- 8¼ x 7-inch piece chipboard
- Photo
- White card stock
- Multicolored striped printed paper
- Large multicolored paper initial
- Date stamp
- Black ink pad
- 2 (¾-inch) silver bulldog clips
- Pink woven alphabet letters to spell "girl"
- Preprinted "100% authentic" twill tape
- Light green ⅜-inch-wide grosgrain ribbon with white pin dots
- Foam brush
- Craft knife
- Fine sandpaper
- Matte-finish decoupage medium

Project note: *Use decoupage medium for glue throughout, applying it with a foam brush.*

Cut window in striped printed paper to accommodate photo, leaving room on left side for large initial and on right side for woven "girl" letters. Adhere striped printed paper to white card stock. Cut a smaller window inside the first, leaving a narrow white card-stock border. Adhere photo behind window.

Trim frame to fit on chipboard; adhere. Let dry. Sand edges with sandpaper.

Adhere large initial to white card stock. Trim around edges, leaving a narrow border. Adhere initial to frame to left of photo. Adhere woven letters down right side of frame to spell "girl." Stamp date on frame below photo. Adhere preprinted twill tape across top of frame; wrap ends around to back and adhere.

Affix bulldog clips to top corners; knot ends of ribbon to bulldog clips for hanger. ■

SOURCES: Printed paper and monogram initial from Basic Grey; date stamp and woven letters from Making Memories; preprinted twill tape from 7gypsies; decoupage medium from Duncan Enterprises.

garden
OF
Life
the
in
you are the rarest of flowers

Garden of Life

Design by MARY AYRES

Inked edges, shiny gold brads and foam tape add texture and variety to a plain wooden frame.

Project note: *Adhere elements using instant-dry paper glue unless instructed otherwise.*

Paint back of frame with white acrylic paint. Paint each side of frame, including inner and outer edges, one of the remaining colors. When dry, sand frame to give it a distressed look.

Cut striped printed paper to fit inside frame; adhere with stripes running horizontally.

For flower, using pattern provided (page 158), cut a 3-inch circle from yellow card stock with decorative-edge scissors. Using pattern provided, cut two leaves from different shades of green card stock with decorative-edge scissors. For grass, cut a 4 x ½-inch strip from the third shade of green card stock; trim top edge only with decorative-edge scissors. Ink edges of flower, leaves and grass with light blue ink pad and dry sponge. With aqua, paint a 3-inch piece of cord for stem.

Using the pattern provided, cut a 2½-inch circle from photo; center and adhere to flower. Punch 1/16-inch holes around edge of photo; set mini brads in holes.

Arrange flower, leaves and grass inside frame; adhere card-stock pieces with double-sided adhesive foam squares. Adhere ends of stem only behind flower and grass with instant-dry paper glue.

Use computer to generate, or hand-print, "you are the rarest of flowers" onto white card stock to fit within an area 1⅞ x ¾ inches. Trim 2½ x 1-inch tag around words; ink edges with light blue ink and dry sponge. Punch ⅛-inch hole in end of tag. Thread blue fiber through hole; tie around flower stem. Adhere tag to right-hand leaf with double-sided adhesive foam squares.

Use computer to generate, or hand-print, "in," "the," "garden," "of" and "life" on different colors of card stock, using a different font for each word. Cut rectangles of varying sizes around words, allowing room for holes in ends; ink edges with light blue ink pad and dry sponge.

Punch 1/16 inch holes in ends of tags; mount mini brads in holes. Adhere tags around upper left corner of frame with double-sided adhesive foam squares. ■

SOURCES: Printed paper from Die Cuts With A View; instant-dry paper glue from Beacon.

PATTERNS ON PAGE 158

MATERIALS

- 8-inch-square wooden shadowbox frame
- Color photo
- Card stock: white, yellow, three shades of green, and five shades to coordinate with printed paper
- Green/yellow/blue striped printed paper
- Acrylic craft paints: white, blue, yellow, pale green, aqua
- Light blue ink pad
- Gold mini brads
- Blue fibers
- Jute cord
- Paintbrush
- Fine sandpaper
- Small dry sponge
- Decorative-edge scissors
- Hole punches: 1/16-inch, ⅛-inch
- Instant-dry paper glue
- Double-sided adhesive foam squares: ¼-inch, ½-inch
- Computer with computer fonts (optional)

Dream

Design by MARY AYRES

Pretty papers and coordinating ribbons accented with metal tags combine in this stylish frame.

MATERIALS

- 8-inch square flat wooden frame with 3-inch-square opening
- Matching 3½-inch photos: 1 color print, 1 black-and-white print
- White card stock
- Pink/green/brown printed papers: green circles, pink typewriter letters, multicolored striped, brown dot
- Pink acrylic craft paint
- Silver oval bookplates: 1¾-inch, 2¼-inch
- 1-inch gold metal flower
- Pink mini brad
- Decorative ribbons: ⅜-inch-wide multicolored polka-dot, ⅝-inch-wide pink/green/brown striped, ¼-inch-wide pink-on-pink gingham checked
- Paintbrush
- Cellophane tape
- Instant-dry paper glue
- Computer with computer fonts (optional)

Paint frame with pink acrylic paint.

Cut 8½-inch-long strips from printed papers as follows: 1½-inch-wide green circles, 2¼-inch-wide pink typewriter letters, 3¼-inch-wide multicolored striped, and 1½-inch-wide brown dots.

Arrange strips facedown from top to bottom in order in which they were cut. Tape strips together along seams to form an 8½-inch square.

Lay frame facedown on taped side of paper square; trace around center opening and outer edges. Cut paper along traced lines; adhere paper to front of frame.

Cut oval from black-and-white photo to fit in 2¼-inch bookplate; adhere to back of bookplate. Thread ⅜-inch-wide polka-dot ribbon through holes in bookplate. Adhere bookplate to frame above upper left corner of center opening. Wrap polka-dot ribbon over seam between green circles and pink typewriter letters printed papers; tie ribbon ends to left of bookplate.

Use computer to generate, or hand-print, "dream" on white card stock to fit in 1¾-inch bookplate; cut oval around word and adhere to back of bookplate. Thread ¼-inch-wide pink gingham checked ribbon through holes in bookplate. Adhere bookplate to frame below lower right corner of center opening. Wrap pink gingham checked ribbon over seam between multicolored striped and brown dots printed papers; tie ribbon ends to right of bookplate.

Wrap and glue ⅝-inch-wide striped ribbon across seam between pink and multicolored striped printed papers. Attach pink mini brad to center of gold flower; adhere flower to striped ribbon on right side of frame. Mount color photo in frame. ■

SOURCES: Printed papers and ribbons from KI Memories; metal flower from Nunn Design; instant-dry paper glue from Beacon.

Animal Prints

Designs by HELEN L. RAFSON

Make a loved one look like the cat's meow in this exotic animal-print frame with wooden button accents.

Cut a 7 x 8¼-inch piece of card stock; cut a 3⅜ x 4¾-inch opening in center.

Cut two 3⅝ x 1½-inch strips and two 4¾ x 1½-inch strips from cheetah printed paper with decorative-edge scissors. Cut four 1⅜ x 1½-inch pieces from zebra printed paper with decorative-edge scissors.

Center shorter cheetah strips across top and bottom of card-stock frame; center longer cheetah strips down sides. Arrange zebra pieces in corners. Position strips so that there are even spaces between strips and edges of card stock. Adhere strips to card-stock frame with paper glue.

Cut two 4-inch pieces of twine; separate pieces into individual strands with a needle. Thread one strand of twine onto needle; thread through buttonholes with ends on front; tie ends in a double knot. Repeat with remaining buttons. Trim twine ends.

Center and adhere buttons to zebra printed paper squares in corners with craft glue.

Center and adhere card-stock frame to acrylic frame with paper glue; insert photo into frame. ■

SOURCE: Paper glue and craft glue from Beacon.

MATERIALS

- 5 x 7-inch acrylic frame
- 5 x 7-inch photograph
- Brown card stock
- Printed papers: zebra, cheetah
- 4 (⅝-inch) flat wooden buttons
- Fine twine
- Large-eye needle
- Decorative-edge scissors
- Paper glue
- Craft glue

CHRISTMAS DAY
1956

Christmas 1956

Design by KATHLEEN PANEITZ

Fabric ribbons strung between metal eyelets protect a treasured photograph mounted on stamped and sanded vintage-look papers.

MATERIALS

- 8½ x 10¼-inch piece of chipboard
- 5 x 7-inch piece of glass
- 3¾ x 5⅝-inch photo
- White card stock
- Printed papers: burgundy/tan striped, light green Christmas carols
- Large snowflake stamp
- Black rub-on transfers: letters and numerals
- White acrylic craft paint
- Sepia ink pad
- 4 silver washer eyelets
- Red-and-green decorative ribbon
- Sewing machine with black thread
- Foam brush
- ⅛-inch hole punch
- Eyelet-setting tool
- Sawtooth hanger
- Fine sandpaper
- Matte-finish decoupage medium

Project note: *Use decoupage medium for glue throughout, applying it with a foam brush.*

Machine-stitch striped and carols printed papers together along one edge with zigzag stitch and black thread. Cut an 11 x 13-inch piece from stitched paper with carols printed paper at top and stitching 4 inches from bottom.

Stamp snowflakes randomly over carols printed paper with white acrylic paint.

Adhere photo to white card stock. Trim around photo leaving a ⅜-inch border. Ink edges of card stock with sepia ink pad. Center and adhere photo to printed-paper background.

Apply rub-on transfer letters to spell "CHRISTMAS DAY" and numerals for desired date to borders of photo. (Position rub-on transfers so that they will not be obscured by ribbons.)

Center and punch matching pairs of ⅛-inch holes through printed-paper background above and below photo, positioning holes approximately ½ inch from top and bottom edges and ½–¾ inch in from sides. Set washer eyelets in holes.

Lay glass over photo. Thread ribbons over glass through holes from top to bottom. Stretch ribbon taut to hold glass in place, adhere ribbon ends to back of background.

Center and affix sawtooth hanger to back of chipboard. Center photo layout on chipboard; adhere. Fold edges over to back; adhere. Sand edges with sandpaper. ■

SOURCES: Printed papers from Rusty Pickle and Autumn Leaves; rub-on transfers from Autumn Leaves; chunky stamp and decoupage medium from Duncan Enterprises; washer eyelets from Creative Impressions.

Rocky Mountain Adventure

Design by SANDRA GRAHAM SMITH

This glossy frame allows scrapbook papers to transform into a faux mosaic, giving you a great way to display your most adventuresome self.

MATERIALS
- 6 x 7½-inch flat white frame
- Photo
- Camping-themed printed paper
- Faux mosaic kit
- Preprinted "adventure" twill tape
- Paintbrush
- Glue

Cover front of frame with faux mosaic grout using a paintbrush. Let dry.

Cut a piece of camping-themed printed paper 5 x 6½ inches. On back of paper, measure and mark entire surface in a grid of ½-inch squares. There will be 130 squares total.

Working with one strip at a time, cut strips of camping-themed printed paper into individual squares. Beginning at top of frame and working down, adhere squares to frame front one by one with faux mosaic glue, spacing the squares evenly across the top of the frame. Leave spaces between individual squares, like a mosaic.

Continue to cover the frame in this manner, discarding any squares that would lie within the opening for the photo. Trim squares even with edges of frame opening as needed.

Apply faux mosaic glaze to each square. Let dry.

Insert photo into frame. Adhere "adventure" preprinted twill tape over lower right corner of frame with glue, trimming tape even with edges of frame. ■

SOURCES: Frame from Plaid/All Night Media; faux mosaic kit from Ranger Industries.

Sweet Baby Brag Book

CONTINUED FROM PAGE 12

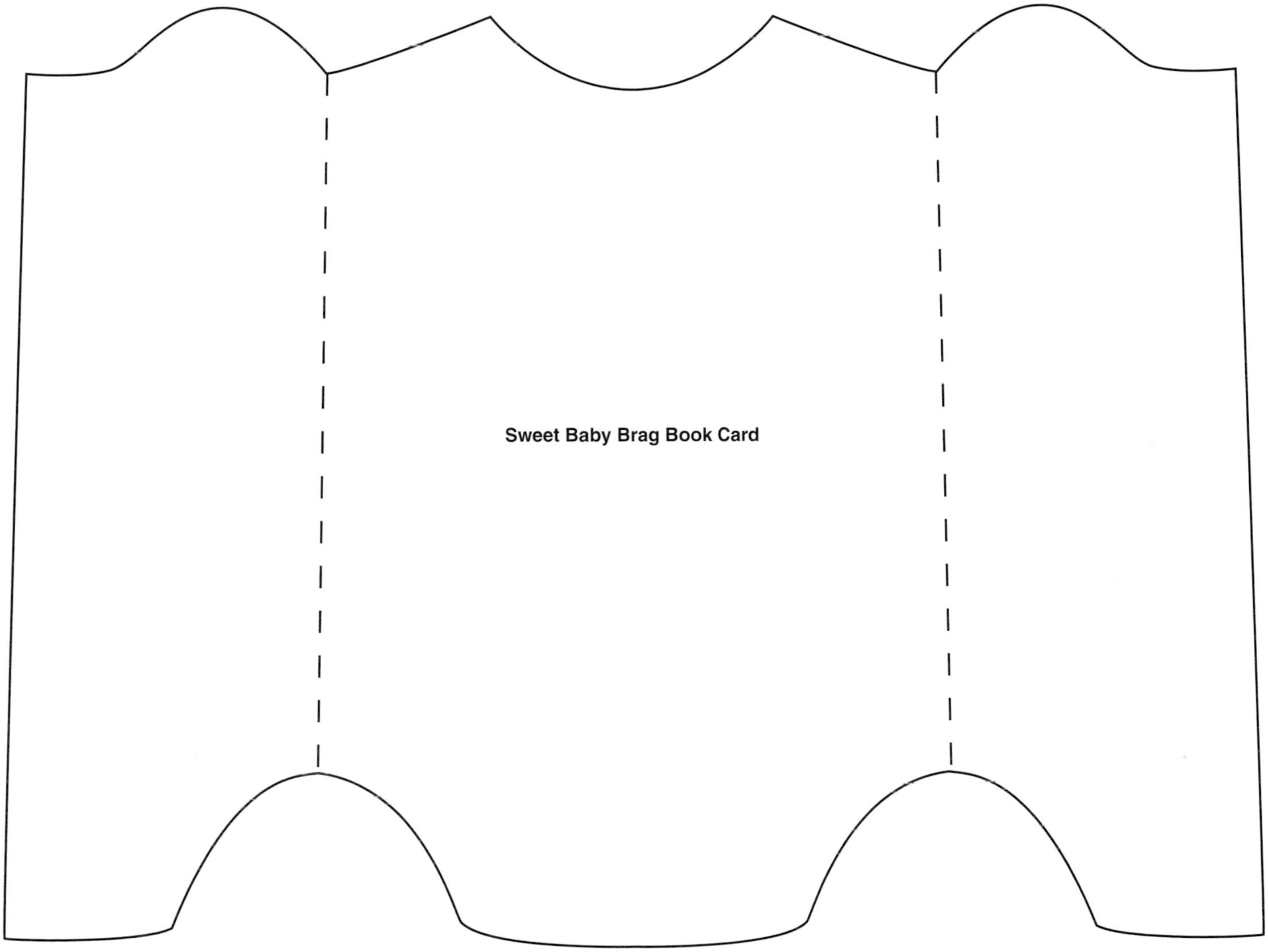

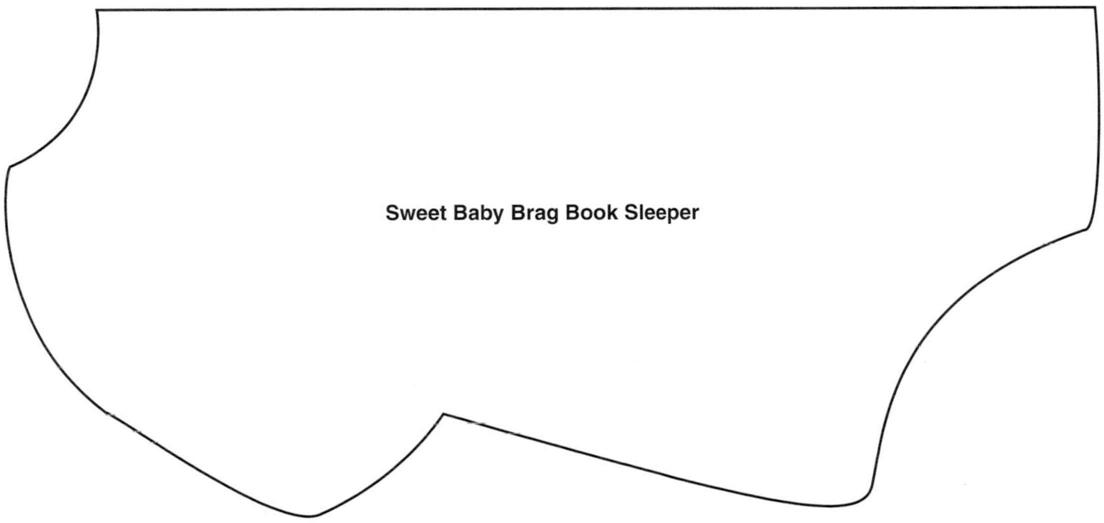

Garden of Life

CONTINUED FROM PAGE 149

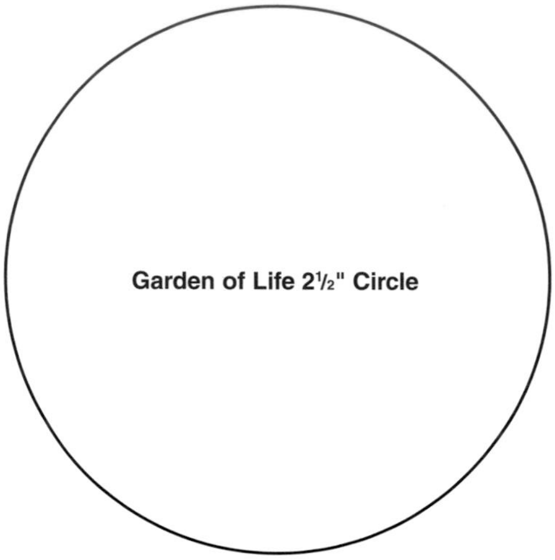

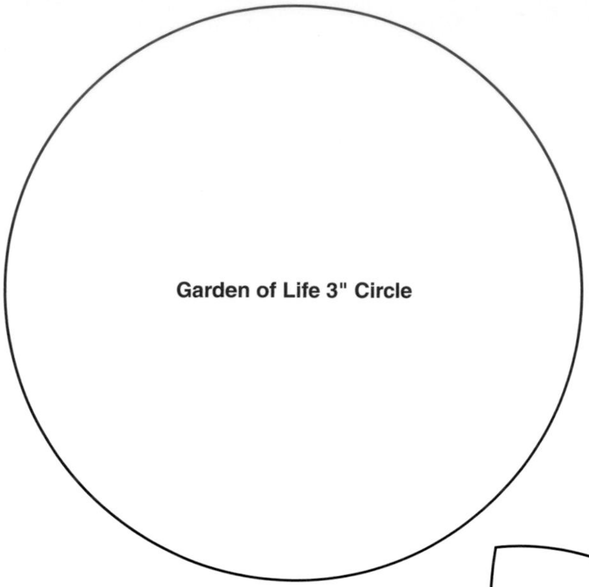

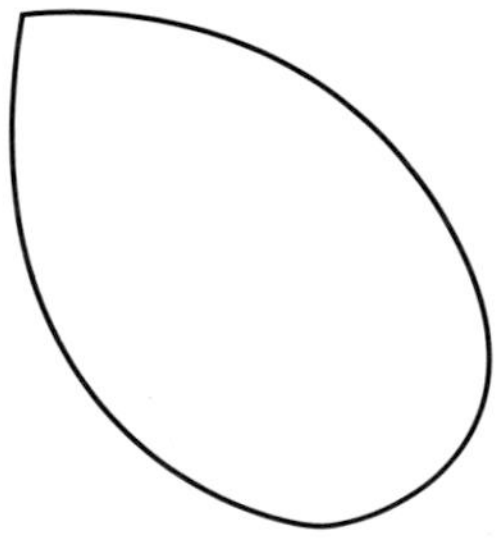

Garden of Life Leaf

Key Ingredients

CONTINUED FROM PAGE 36

Daddy's Little Girl

CONTINUED FROM PAGE 90

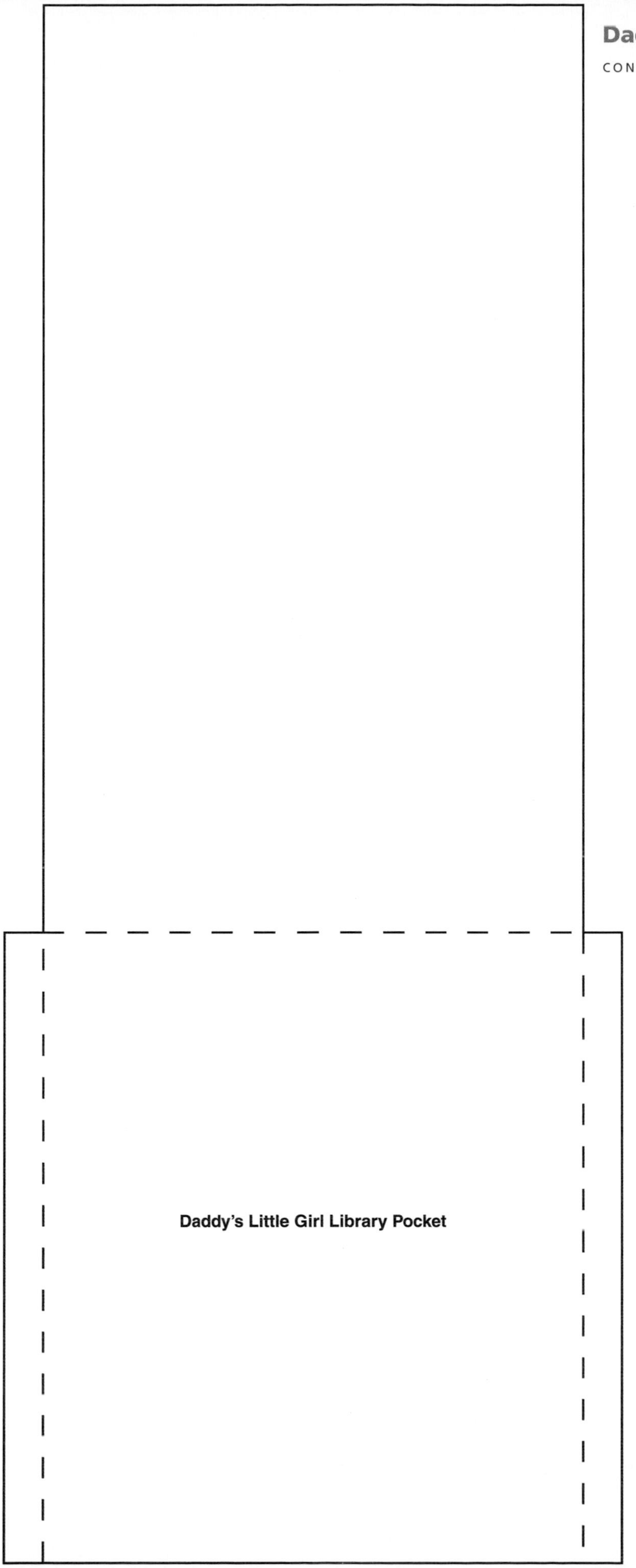

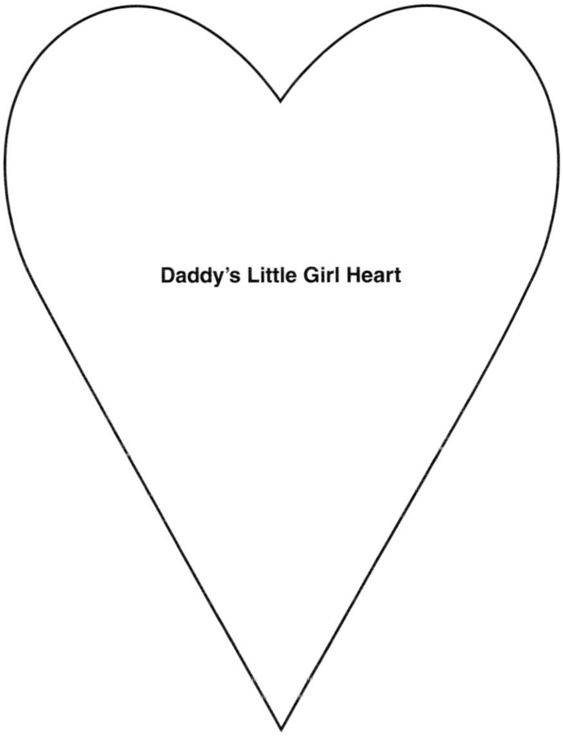

"Sara" Tin

CONTINUED FROM PAGE 59

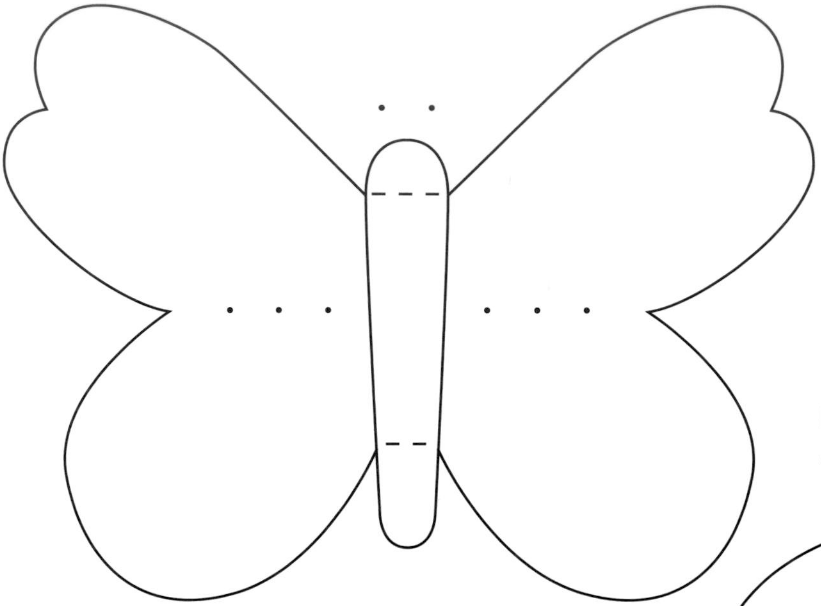

Sara Tin Butterfly Wings

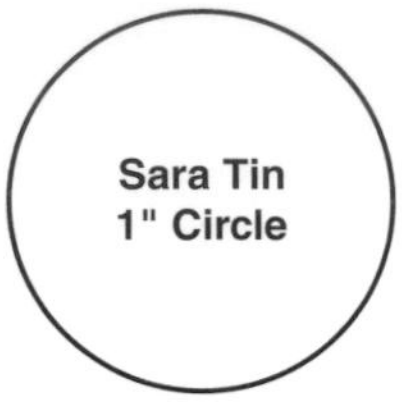

Heritage Tag

CONTINUED FROM PAGE 95

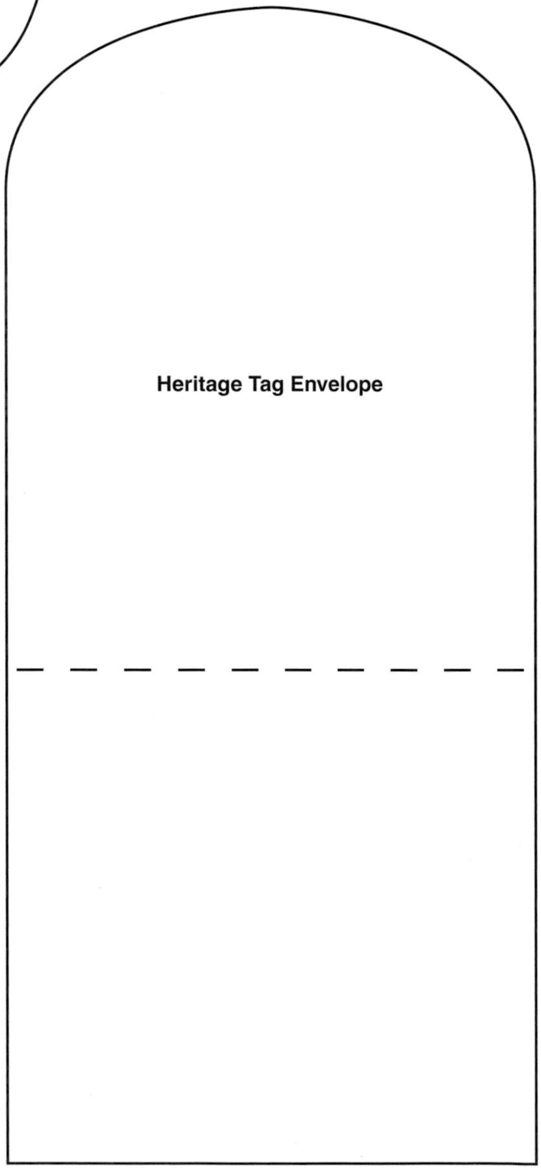

Easter Moments & Memories

CONTINUED FROM PAGE 117

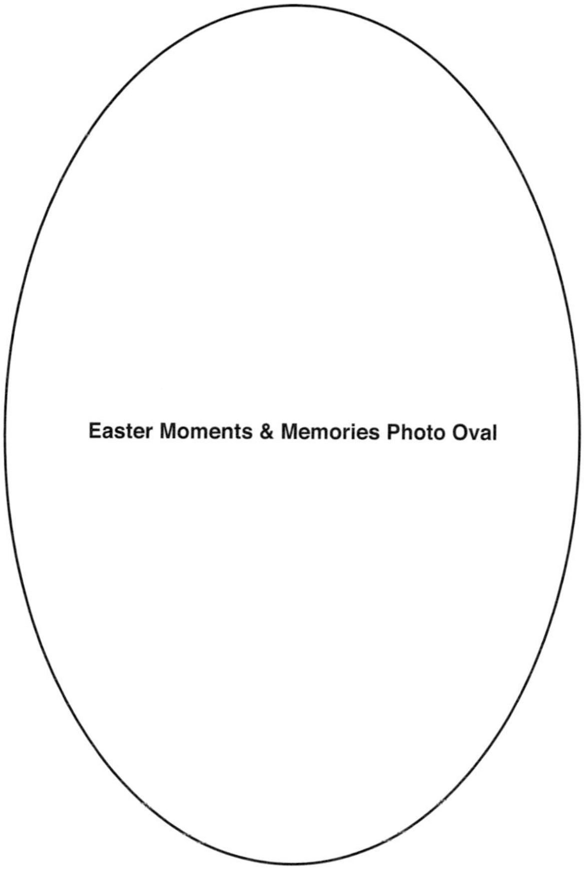

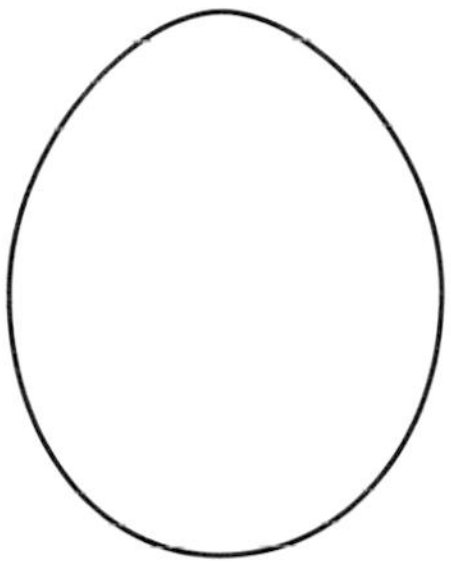

Easter Moments & Memories
Easter Egg

Easter Moments & Memories
Easter Egg Stripe

Here's Looking at You, Kid

CONTINUED FROM PAGE 136

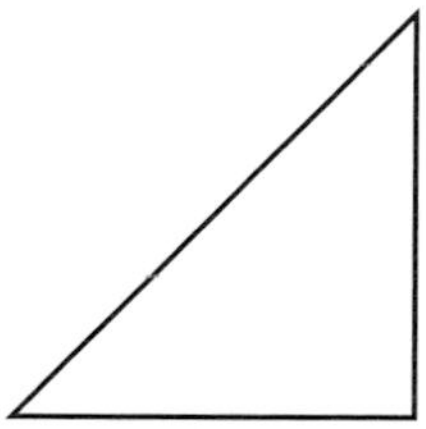

"Here's Looking at You, Kid" Corner

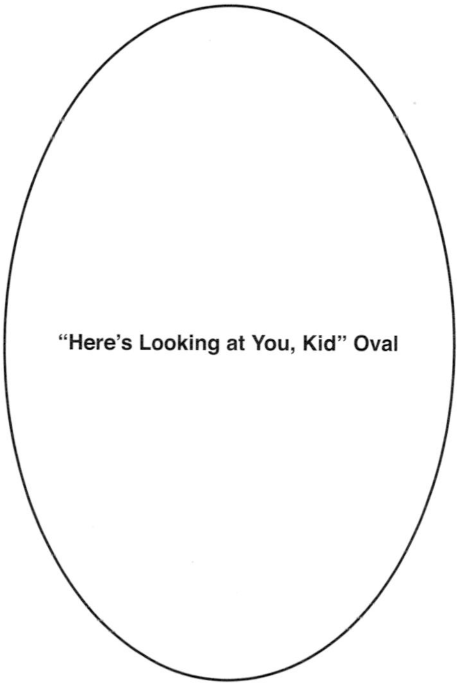

Crafting With Photos

By MARIA NERIUS

Introduction

If a picture is worth a thousand words, then the projects you can create with your photos are priceless! Don't leave your pictures in a shoebox or put them on a shelf to sort through someday. Use those wonderful photographs to create something grand.

You can have fun with photo transferring, organizing a photo mosaic, colorizing a black-and-white photo to capture the romance of years gone by, and even creating an interesting collage to celebrate your life. The power of the visual medium of photography is made extra special when you add the spirit of creativity. Get out those photos and start a project that will be enjoyed by everyone!

Handy Tools

The list of photo-crafting tools could go on forever, but there are a few that are vital for any project. The first is a sharp cutting tool, which can be traditional scissors, a personal trimmer or a craft knife. It is important that you always work with tools that are sharp. A dull cutting blade or pair of scissors can tear or mar a photo—especially photos that are printed on home printers. These are very functional tools and a must for photo crafting.

Cutting tools can also be just plain fun! There are dozens of decorative scissors, hand paper punches and die-cutting plates to help you create interesting, exciting edges and corners for your photos. You can choose from deckled edges to postage-stamp edges to traditional zigzag edges to add variety to your projects. Paper punches come in every size and shape from apples to zebras! Dies can usually be found at craft or scrapbook stores where you pay per cut of the die. Dies are available in even more shapes and sizes than hand punches.

Adhesives are important to any craft project. It's best to coordinate the adhesive to the materials you are using. Photos can be attached in a variety of ways, from liquid glue to any of the many types of tape that are available. If you are adhering anything heavy or nonporous to your photo project, you'll need to consider a specialty paper glue or a jewelry glue, both of which are designed to hold heavier items to a surface. Many artists and crafters are incorporating metal and glass into their photo crafts, and this technique calls for a stronger glue. If you are only working with lightweight embellishments and paper, then most white glues will do the trick. Archival,

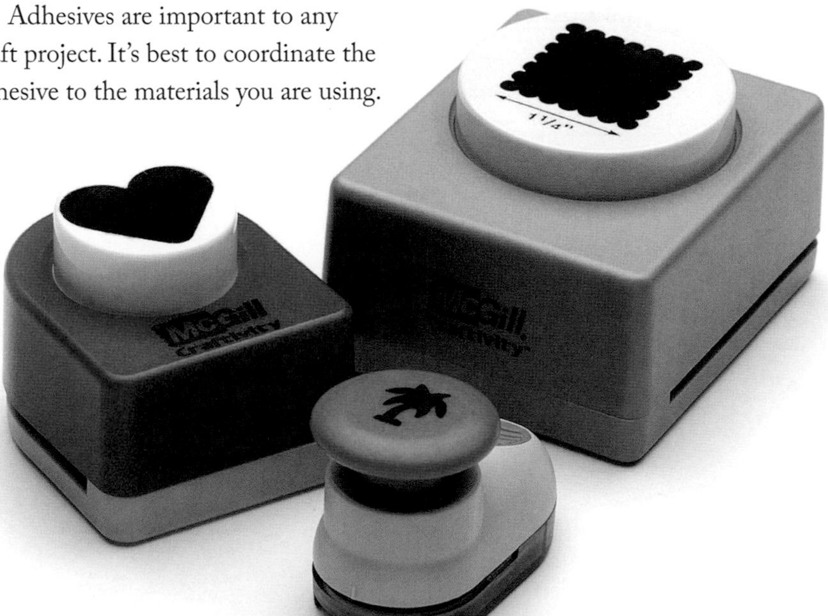

heirloom and scrapbooking projects should use a glue labeled as acid-free to prevent eventual deterioration of the photographs.

Pens, inks, colored or watercolor pencils, markers, chalk and paint all add color and interest to photo crafts. Feel free to use them with splash and flash; however, if creating an archival or heirloom design, keep in mind that there are acid-free pens, colored pencils, inks, markers and paint available. Most of these supplies are indeed acid-free, but not all manufacturers go through the testing process. Call the manufacturer if you have archival-quality questions. The same goes for most printer inks; most are acid-free, but are not always labeled as such.

Other handy tools include stencils and templates. A huge variety of clever and inspiring stencils and templates are available at art and craft–supply stores, and a quick search on the Internet will provide dozens of free stencils and templates to choose from. You can cut an interesting shape, emboss a raised image and fold a beautiful flower, all with the help of these tools.

Just a Reminder

You probably have a few older photographs in your collection. It is important to remember that if the photo doesn't have a negative, you might want to craft with a copy of that photo, not the original. Old photos with charming sepia tones or hand tinting are great to craft with, but often are one-of-a-kind family mementoes. Keep the original photograph intact and make a few copies to craft with.

Digital or the Old-Fashioned Way?

It doesn't really matter anymore if you use photos taken with film or photos printed at home from your digital camera. The key is getting the best quality print you can. If you are working with an actual photograph rather than a photocopied print, you need quality photo paper and a quality printer. Photo paper is easy to find for home printers, but home printer quality still doesn't quite match that of a commercial photo developer. You need to decide what you prefer for each individual project you undertake.

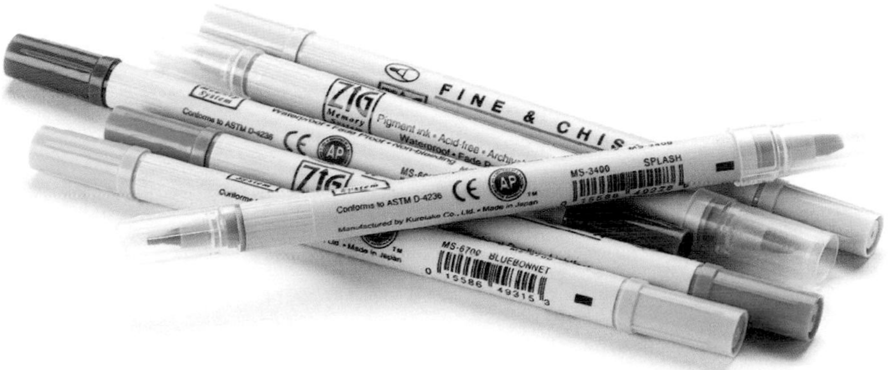

Sometimes a photo print from your home computer system is fine, while there may be other projects for which you'll prefer to have a professionally printed photo.

Tips for Photographs

To create great photo craft projects, you need to start with great photos! Here are some tips that leading professional photographers pass along to camera enthusiasts.

1 Know your camera. Read your camera manual and refer to it if you have any problems. It is very important that you know what all the buttons do and what features are available. Most are there for a good reason and to give you the best possible photos. The next step is to practice and keep your camera handy for any photo opportunity.

2 Do more than just aim and click your camera. Take charge and get the photo you want. As you look through the viewfinder, take time to really see what you are looking at. Ask people to move closer together for a better shot. Tell Grandpa Ralph to lean slightly to the left or right. Add a prop. Remove a hat. Do whatever it takes to make the photo better, tell a story or make you smile.

3 The most vital part of every photograph you take is light. Lighting affects the appearance of everything you photograph. Harsh light can make your subjects squint and grimace. Not enough light results in shadowy darkness. If the lighting is not right, move yourself or your subject. Check the settings on your camera and adjust for bright light, cloudiness, incandescent or fluorescent light, and moonlight.

Learn when to use your flash to fill in with supplemental light and when you should use the red-eye reducer. According to a leading camera manufacturer, the No. 1 flash mistake is taking pictures beyond the range of

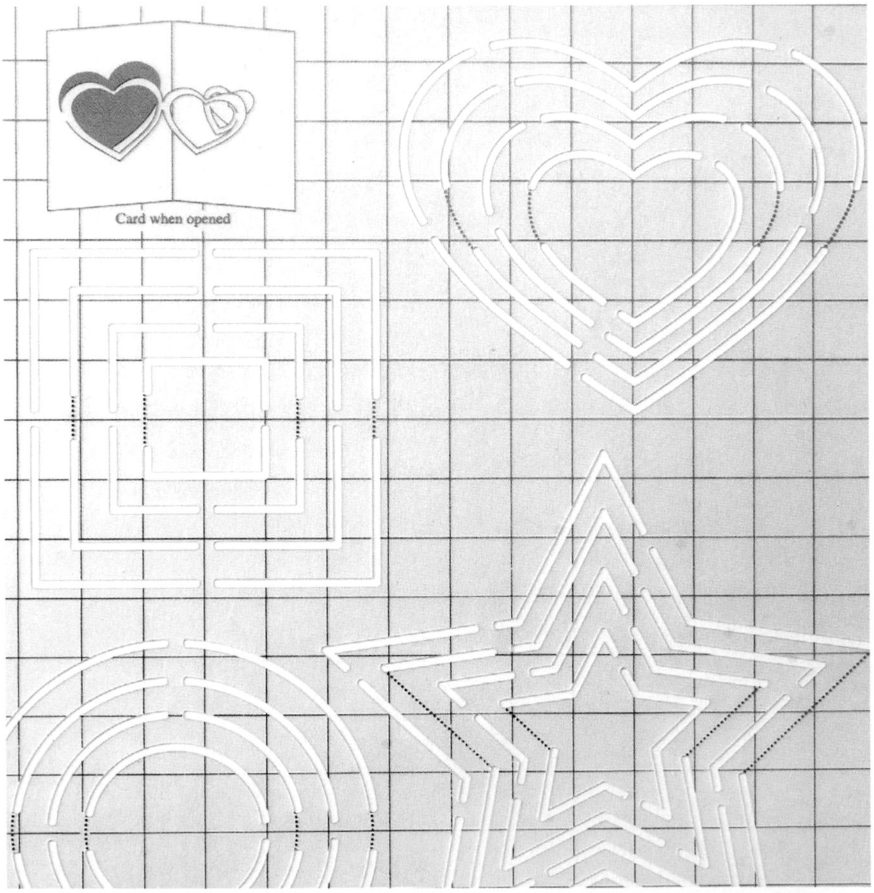

the flash. Photos taken beyond the maximum flash range will be too dark. As a general rule most cameras have a maximum flash range of less than 15 feet. You can find the flash range in the camera manual.

4 Get down (or up) to the photo subject's eye level. This is especially important when photographing children and pets. You may have to kneel, bend, hunch or stand on a stool, but the effort is worth it. Being at eye level gives a warm, personal feel to the photo without the necessity of the subject looking directly at the camera lens. In fact, some of the most intimate photos are those with the subject looking off to either side of the camera lens.

5 When you look through the camera viewfinder, it is natural for you to focus all of your attention on the subject. However, your camera is not doing the same. Standing too far away can lead to your subject getting lost in the landscape or background. Move closer so you can see more detail. Or, if your camera has a zoom lens, let the camera do the work by zooming closer. Next time you take a picture of your best friend, let her face fill the viewfinder and you'll get some amazing results.

6 Hold the camera steady with both hands and gently push the shutter button down. Nothing can blur a great photo faster than unsteady hands. Consider using a tripod for posed shots.

7 Most photos are taken with a horizontal frame. It's natural and done without thinking. Why not shoot a photo vertically every now and then? Many things look better when a vertical picture is taken, such as friends standing around a birthday cake, or tall buildings. This adds variety to the photos by showing different lines, shapes, forms and perspective. Next time you get ready to shoot a photo, take a few extra seconds and turn your camera sideways. You might get a better shot.

8 A plain background gives focus to the subject you are photographing. When you look through the camera viewfinder, learn to pay attention to the area surrounding your subject. Make sure no trees grow from the head of your grandson and no wires seem to be stretching from the sides of Aunt Barb. Keep your photo backgrounds free from clutter.

9 To avoid the dreaded bull's-eye syndrome, remember the rule of thirds. Divide your photo frame into nine equal segments. Instead of having the focus of your photo in the center of the nine squares, place it off-center in any of the remaining eight. If you photograph the horizon

Did You Know?

• *People immediately look at another human in a photo* even if the person is very small in the frame. Our attention will go to anything *alive* as opposed to something inanimate. The hierarchy of attention is humans over animals, animals over plants.

• *Colors draw our attention* and the warm shades of red, yellow and orange will jump out of a background of cool-tone colors like blue and green. Even a small subject will dominate if it's different from its surroundings. It could be its color, brightness or the direction it's facing. Anything that's isolated from everything else will draw attention to itself.

• *No matter what else* is in the scene, the eye is irresistibly drawn to the lightest, brightest area. That's why any bright blob of light or bit of paper in the background is distracting. All other things being equal, the eye will go to the area of highest contrast. The eye will go to the subject that's in sharpest focus.

• *Can you crop Polaroid photographs?* Yes and no! Cutting an older Polaroid photograph releases harmful chemicals from inside the image. As an alternative, you can place a frame made of acid-free paper over the top of the photograph, hiding the white borders. According to the manufacturer, photos made from film manufactured after 2003 can be cut without problems.

line at the bottom third of your frame, the focus of the photo will be the magnificent sunset. If the horizon line is at the top third of the camera frame, the focus will be the craggy mountains, with the sunset as an accent. The same rule applies to photographing people or pets. Keeping the subject a bit off-center adds to the variety of lines, shapes, forms, balance and harmony of the photograph, which in turn will create more exciting photos for your craft projects.

10 Black-and-white photos are known to have a longer life than most color photographs and are often more dramatic, so include black-and-white film in your picture taking. Some digital cameras have a black-and-white (grayscale) mode. You also have an opportunity to include black-and-white style when you scan a photo by using photo-editing software that includes a grayscale feature.

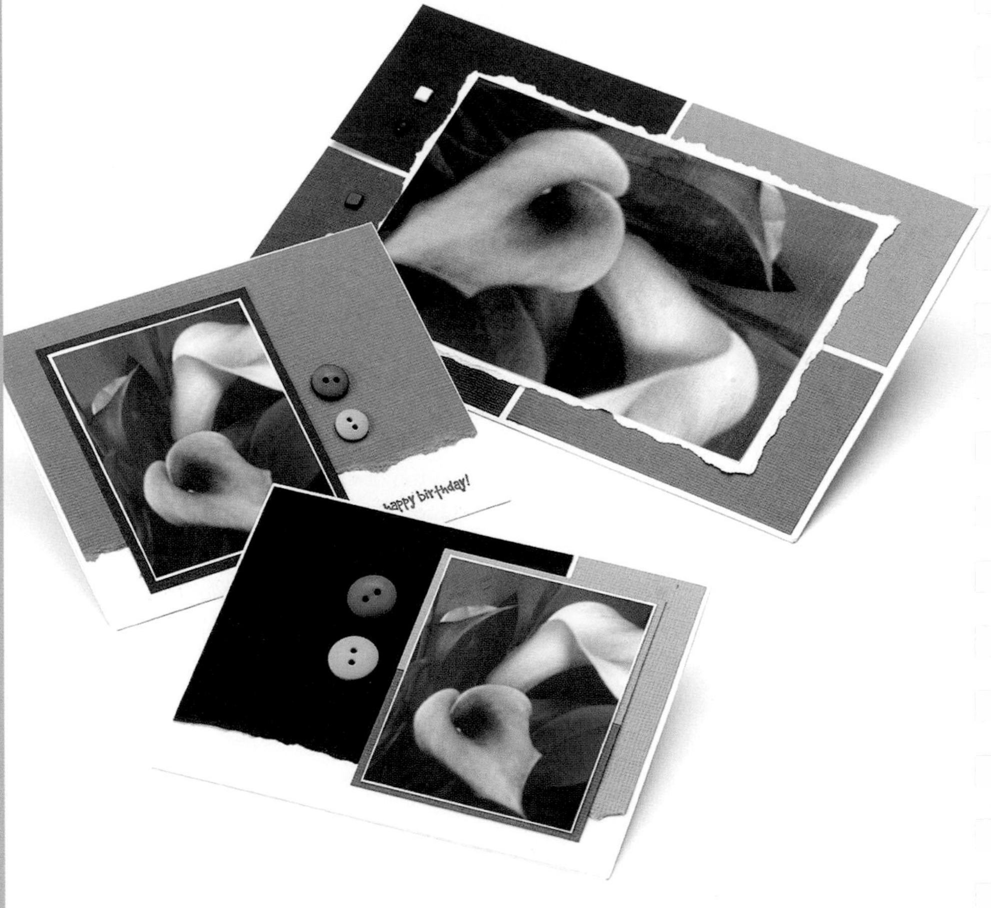

Adding Color to a Black-and-White Photo

Coloring a black-and-white photo can add a special tint to your photo crafts. It is not as hard as you might imagine it to be. The finished effect is nostalgic and romantic. You may find some original hand-colored photos among your older treasured family photos. These photos were probably hand-colored by professional photographers using oil paints. This technique is still used, and oil-paint products are available at art, craft and photography shops. However, modern products have taken much of the tedium and mystery out of this technique. You no longer have to be a professional artist or even have any artistic ability to hand-color photos.

The first rule to remember is never hand-color an original black-and-white photo. Have a copy made on photo paper. Remember that any negative can be developed into a black-and-white photo, and a color photo can be printed in black and white at a photo developer or by using your computer.

That's right, even your color negatives can be processed into black-and-white photos. Once the film has been developed, just ask your developer to make some copies in black-and-white. Most shops will not be able to do this process in-house, but it is well worth the extra day or two it takes to obtain black-and-white prints to hand-color.

There are three basic methods used to hand-color an actual photo. The first involves an oil paint, as previously described. This method takes some practice and the paint is applied by brush or paint pen. The second method uses acrylic paint or tints and is applied in the same manner. The final method, and by far the easiest, is to use markers specifically developed to hand-color black-and-white photos. Depending on what brand of products is used, you may have to sponge a solution

onto the photo to soften the top layer, making it more receptive to color. You'll then apply the color. You may have to use an aerosol finish on the photo once completed to preserve the color.

Photo-coloring markers provide very transparent tinting. Add color in a circular motion, and apply layer upon layer of color until the desired intensity is reached. Experiment with different colors. Many manufacturers carry stock colors that are close to the original hues used by professionals in days of old. Many manufacturers also include modern colors in their palettes.

You can also use colored pencils to add soft color to photos. Photocopy the print (if it is a black-and-white print, copy it on a color copier to get richer gray tones), then add subtle strokes to add touches of color. If you have your print copied onto a heavy card stock or watercolor paper (printable watercolor papers are available at most art or computer stores), you can also use watercolor pencils to give the effect of hand-coloring. You'll softly stroke color into one area of the image and then,

What's With the Paper?

Paper is a wonderful medium to use in photo crafting, but not all paper is the same. Here is a quick review of some papers you might like to use while creating with your photos.

Acetate: thin, flexible sheet of transparent plastic

Board: paper generally used for file folders, displays and postcards

Bond: paper generally used for writing, printing and photocopying

Buffered: made in an acid environment and then buffered on the surface to obtain a required pH

Cardboard: general term for stiff, bulky paper such as index, tag or Bristol

Coated: papers with a finish or coating that can be glossy or matte

Corrugated: fluted paper between sheets of paper or cardboard, or the fluted paper by itself

Dry gum: label paper or sheet of paper with glue on one side that can be activated by water

Handmade: sheet of paper made individually by hand using a mold and deckle

Index: lightweight board paper for writing and easy erasure

Mulberry: Made from the Sa-tree, this handmade paper contains coarse fibers that create a feathery look when the paper is torn or ripped.

Origami: very lightweight paper designed to crease or fold well

Parchment: paper that imitates writing "papers" made from animal skins

Quilling: lightweight paper, usually brightly colored, cut into very thin strips that are rolled into coils and shaped

Rice: A misnomer that is applied to lightweight Oriental papers, the name may be derived from the rice sizing once used in Japanese papermaking.

Tissue: thin, translucent, lightweight paper

Vellum: stiff, translucent paper available clear, colored, printed or embossed

Velveteen: paper with velvet nap and feel

Watercolor: Hot press is used for stamping because it is smooth; cold press is bumpy and is used mostly for painting. It has a high wet strength, meaning it doesn't lose strength when water is absorbed.

Waterleaf: paper with little or no sizing, making it very absorbent

using a small damp paintbrush or waterbrush, you'll add just a touch of water to allow the pencil color to flow or blend, as watercolors do so beautifully.

Magical Mosaics

You've probably seen beautiful mosaics used to create stepping-stones, tabletops, candleholders and wall art, but did you ever think of creating a mosaic with your photos? Somehow all the little pieces add up to big results! You can create your own mosaic by selecting the photos you want to include. Decide on how big you want each "tile" to be and start cutting! Large or small pieces do give different effects, so you may want to look through some photo-crafting books or do an Internet search for inspiration.

Give yourself plenty of working area, as you will want to keep some kind of order to the photo pieces. Once you have enough photos cut to fill in your surface you can start gluing. Use a paper glue or double-sided tape. Leave a hint of a border or space between the photo pieces as you adhere each to a heavyweight background paper. You can use several photos or have a single photo enlarged. If you don't feel comfortable enough to "wing it" on your own, there are photo mosaic templates available at craft, scrapbooking and Internet stores. Photos take on a different feel when cut up and then pieced together again.

Weave an Image

Weaving with strips from a photo is a unique way to add dimension and pattern to a photo-crafting design. Most of us learned the basics of weaving in grade school while creating place mats and Valentine hearts that only our moms could really appreciate! The easiest technique to learn (or relearn) is the process of "over one, under one."

Here are a few weaving terms to become familiar with:

Loom—the frame used for weaving the piece.

Warp—the pieces that run from top to bottom (up and down).

Weft—the pieces than run across the *warp* (side to side).

Web—the single or whole piece created by weaving.

You'll need two identical photos, a personal trimmer or craft knife with ruler and self-healing cutting mat, and adhesive. The first photo will act as the loom as well as the warp. On the back of the photo, measure and mark ¼ inch, ½ inch or 1 inch (depending on the size of the photo) from what will be the top and both sides. Do not cut beyond these marks or your loom will fall apart. The warp pieces can be cut straight or curved, with all of them the same width or different widths. Cut the weft strips from the second photo (straight or curved). To make it easier, you can draw and number the curved pieces on the back before cutting them.

Begin weaving the first row by placing one strip of weft over one warp and under the next warp, and repeat to the end of the row. The second row starts with placing a weft strip under one warp and over the next warp; repeat to the end of the row. Keep the weft strips pushed toward the top of the loom. Alternate row one and row two until the web is complete. Secure woven ends with a touch of glue. Now you are ready to use your woven photo as is or as an element of scrapbooking, card making, paper art, collage and other fun creations.

Wild & Wacky Effects

If you enjoy working with a computer, many software programs with photo-editing applications include a wonderful creative tool called a filter. The filter can be applied to an entire image or part of an image. Filters can be fairly simple effects used to mimic traditional photographic filters (which are pieces of colored glass or gelatine placed over the lens to absorb specific wavelengths of light), or they can be complex programs used to create astounding artistic effects. Using filters is a creative way to alter photos for crafting.

Original snapshot

Glass filter

Canvas filter

You can create 3-D effects, instant sepia or aging, watercolor, colored foil, kaleidoscope or even a linen texture for your photos, all with a click of a mouse! The photos can be printed out on a variety of surfaces including watercolor paper, fabric, acetate transparencies, handmade paper, specialty papers and, of course, photo paper. Most software allows you to temporarily apply the filter to your scanned or digital photo so that you can see if you like it before saving it as a permanent file. Remember to always keep the original file untouched. You can do this by saving the filtered photo under a different file name.

Delightful Decoupage

This traditional technique can be applied to photo crafting with excellent results. You can decoupage a photo or a photocopied photo. Make sure when you are using photocopies that you always test a small area of the photocopy to make sure the ink is permanent.

Decoupage is traditionally done by adhering a print (in this case a photo) to a surface, usually wood. The wooden piece should be well prepared by sanding away rough edges and making sure all dust and dirt is wiped away. You'll also need a paintbrush, decoupage medium or sealer.

Apply a thin film of the decoupage medium to the wooden surface and place the photo on top. Gently press the photo, making sure there are no bumps, wrinkles or air bubbles underneath. Apply a second coat of decoupage medium, covering the entire surface, including the top of the photo.

Sepia filter

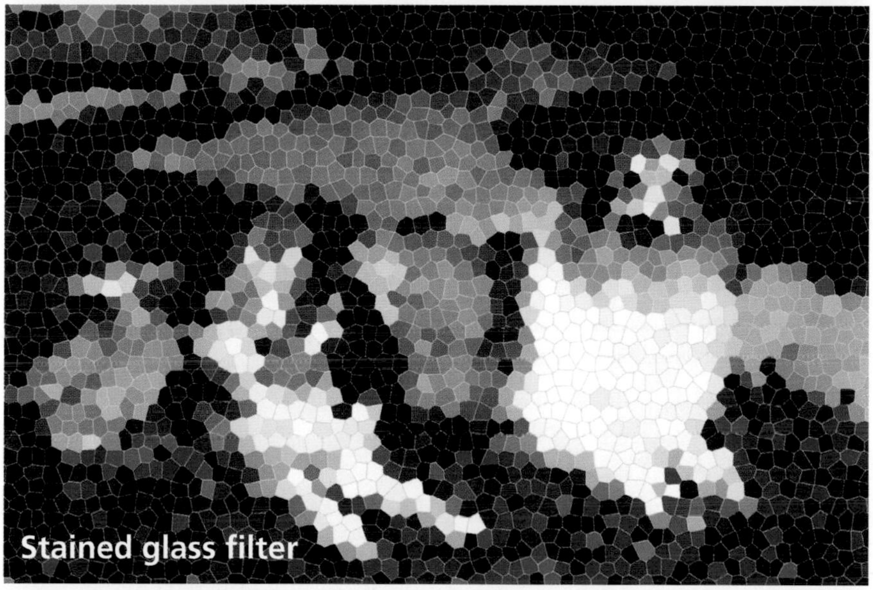

Stained glass filter

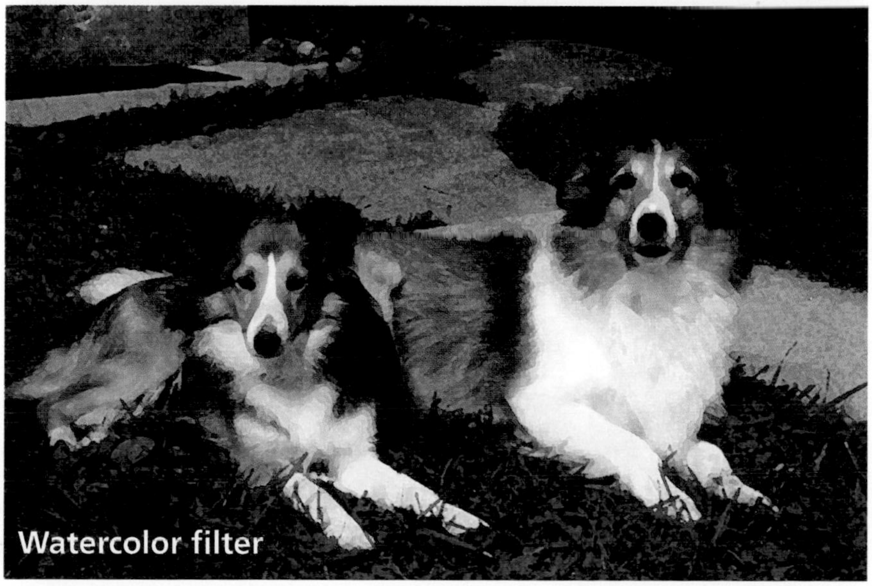

Watercolor filter

Add several more coats of decoupage medium, allowing each coat to dry completely.

Decoupage can also be applied to paper and glass surfaces, but decoupage medium will not permanently adhere to most plastics.

Copyright Issues

Thinking of selling your photo crafts? If using your own photos that have been taken by you, a friend or someone in your family, you have nothing to worry about when it comes to copyright laws. Professional photographers, however, own all the rights to photographs (even though you have purchased the photographs themselves), and you may not use their photographs for commercial use. In other words, you may not sell for profit anything using their photos. You must request permission from a photographer to use a photo and you must get a release form from him or her to do so.

General Instructions

Paper crafting is easy, creative and fun. Collect basic tools and supplies, learn a few simple terms and techniques, and you're ready to start. The possibilities abound!

Cutting & Tearing

Craft knife, cutting mat Must-have tools. Mat protects work surface, keeps blades from getting dull.

Measure and mark Diagrams show solid lines for cutting, dotted lines for folding.

Other cutters Guillotine and rotary-blade paper cutters, oval and circle cutters, cutters that cut unusual shapes via a gear or cam system, swivel-blade knives that cut along the channels of plastic templates, and die-cutting machines (large or small in size and price). Markers that draw as they cut.

Punches Available in hundreds of shapes and sizes ranging from 1/16 inch to over 3 inches (use for eyelets, lettering, dimensional punch art and embellishments). Also punches for two-ring, three-ring, coil, comb and disk binding.

Scissors Long and short blades that cut straight or a pattern. Scissors with nonstick coating are ideal for cutting adhesive sheets and tape. Bonsai scissors are best for cutting rubber or heavy board. Consider comfort—large holes for fingers, soft grips.

Tearing Tear paper for collage, special effects, layering on cards, scrapbook pages and more. Wet a small paintbrush with water then brush across paper where tear is desired; tear along the wet line for a deckle edge.

Embellishments

If you are not already a pack rat, it is time to start! Embellish projects with stickers, eyelets, brads, nail heads, wire, beads, iron-on ribbon and braid, memorabilia and printed ephemera.

Embossing

Dry embossing Use a light source, stencil, card stock and stylus tool. Add color, or leave raised areas plain.

Heat embossing Use embossing powder, ink, card stock and a heat tool to create raised designs and textures. Powders come in a wide range of colors. Fine grain is called "detail" and heavier is called "ultrathick." Embossing powders will not stick to most dye inks—use pigment inks or special clear embossing inks for best results.

Glues & Adhesives

Basics Each glue or adhesive is formulated for a particular use and specified surfaces. Read the label and carefully follow directions, especially those that involve personal safety and health.

Foam tape Adds dimension.

Glue dots, adhesive sheets and cartridge type machines Quick grab, no drying time needed.

Glue pens Fine-line control.

Glue sticks Wide coverage.

Repositionable products Useful for stencils and temporary holding.

Measuring

Rulers A metal straightedge for cutting with a craft knife (a must-have tool). Match the length of the ruler to the project (shorter rulers are easier to use when working on smaller projects).

Quilter's grid ruler Use to measure squares and rectangles.

Pens & Markers

Choose inks (permanent, watercolor, metallic, etc.), **colors** (sold by sets or individually), **and nibs** (fine point, calligraphy, etc.) **to suit the project.** For journals and scrapbooks, make sure inks are permanent and fade-resistant.

Store pens and markers flat unless the manufacturer says otherwise.

Scoring & Folding

Folding Mountain folds—up, valley folds—down. Most patterns will have different types of dotted lines to denote mountain or valley folds.

Tools Scoring tool and bone folder. Fingernails will scar the surface of the paper.

Paper & Card Stock

Card stock Heavier and stiffer than paper. A sturdy surface for cards, boxes, ornaments.

Paper Lighter-weight surfaces used for drawing, stamping, collage.

Storage and organization Store paper flat and away from moisture. Arrange by color, size or type. Keep your scraps for collage projects.

Types Handmade, milled, marbled, mulberry, origami, embossed, glossy, matte, botanical inclusions, vellum, parchment, preprinted, tissue and more.

Stamping

Direct-to-paper (DTP) Use ink pad, sponge or stylus tool to apply ink instead of a rubber stamp.

Inks Available in pads and re-inker bottles. Types include dye and pigment, permanent, waterproof and fade resistant or archival, chalk finish, fast drying, slow drying, rainbow and more. Read the labels to determine what is best for a project or surface.

Make stamps Carve rubber, erasers, carving blocks, vegetables. Heat Magic Stamp foam blocks to press against textures. Stamp found objects such as leaves and flowers, keys and coins, etc.

Stamps Sold mounted on wood, acrylic or foam, or unmounted (rubber part only), made from vulcanized rubber, acrylic or foam.

Store Flat and away from light and heat.

Techniques Tap the ink onto the stamp (using the pad as the applicator) or tap the stamp onto the ink pad. Stamp with even hand pressure (no rocking) for best results. For very large stamps, apply ink with a brayer. Color the surface of a stamp with watercolor markers (several colors), huff with breath to keep the colors moist, then stamp; or lightly spray with water mist before stamping for a very different effect.

Unmounted stamps Mount temporarily on acrylic blocks with Scotch Poster Tape on one surface (nothing on the rubber stamp) or one of the other methods (hook-and-loop fastener, paint-on adhesives, cling plastic).

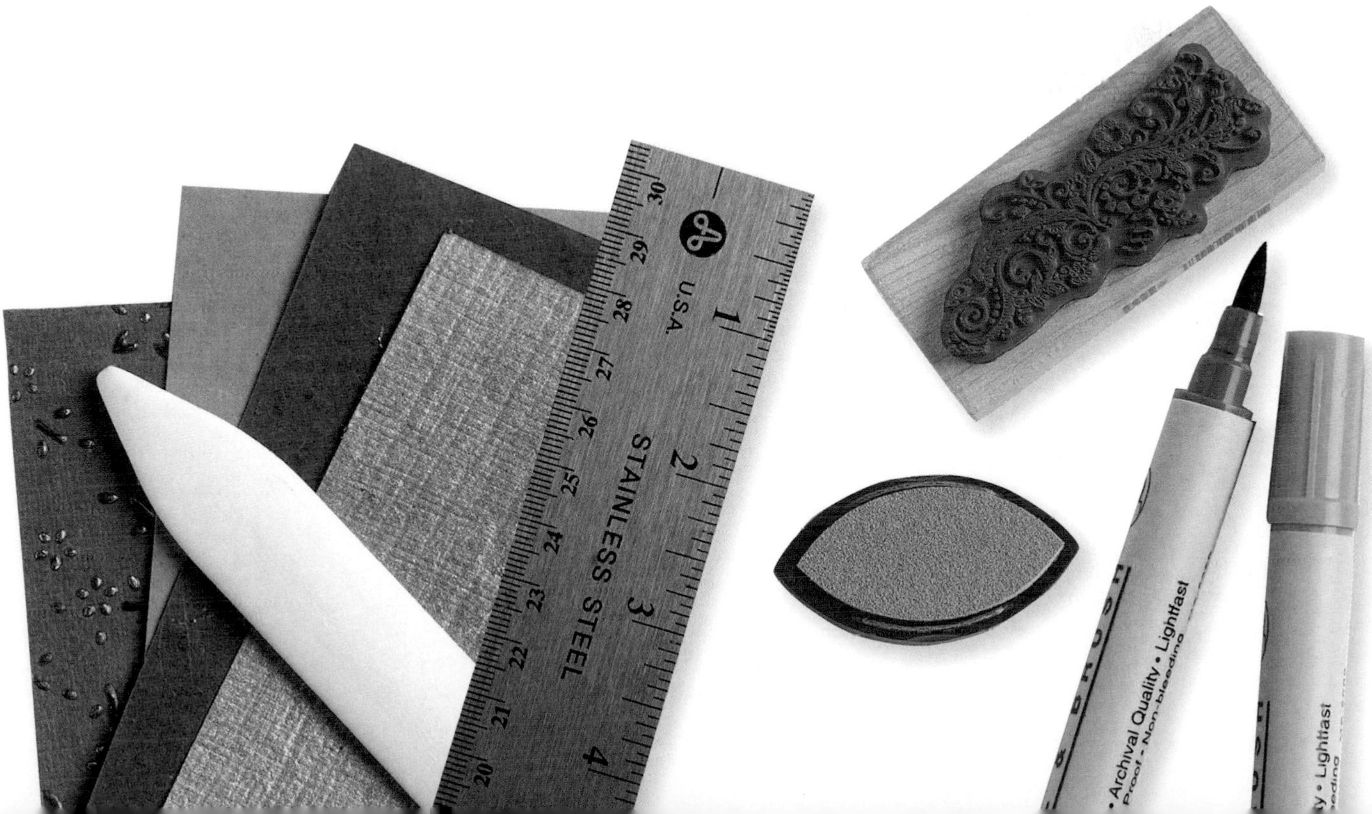

BUYER'S GUIDE

Projects in this book were made using products provided by the manufacturers listed below. Look for the suggested products in your local craft- and art-supply stores. If unavailable, contact suppliers below. Some may be able to sell products directly to you; others may be able to refer you to retail sources.

7gypsies
(877) 749-7797
www.sevengypsies.com

AccuCut
(800) 288-1670
www.accucut.com

All My Memories
(888) 553-1998
www.allmymemories.com

Altered Pages
(405) 360-1185
www.alteredpages.com

Anna Griffin Inc.
(888) 817-8170
www.annagriffin.com

Arctic Frog
(479) 636-3764
www.arcticfrog.com

Autumn Leaves
(800) 588-6707
www.autumnleaves.com

Authentic Models Inc.
www.authenticmodels.com

Avery
www.avery.com

A.W. Cute
(877) 560-6943
www.awcute.com

BasicGrey
(801) 544-1116
www.basicgrey.com

Bazzill Basics Paper
(480) 558-8557
www.bazzillbasics.com

Beacon Adhesives Inc.
(914) 699-3400
www.beaconcreates.com

The Beadery
(401) 539-2432
www.thebeadery.com

Board Dudes
(800) 521-4332
www.boarddudes.com

Boxer Scrapbook Productions
(888) 625-6255
www.boxerscrapbooks.com

Carolee's Creations & Co.
(435) 563-1100
www.caroleescreations.com

Chatterbox
(888) 416-6260
www.chatterboxinc.com

Clearsnap Inc.
(888) 448-4862
www.clearsnap.com

Close To My Heart
www.closetomyheart.com

Cloud 9 Design
(763) 493-0990
www.cloud9design.biz

C.M. Offray & Son Inc.
www.offray.com

Colorbök
(734) 424-0505
www.colorbok.com

Color Workshop
www.ColorWorkshop.com

Creative Imaginations
(800) 942-6487
www.cigift.com

Creative Impressions
(719) 596-4860
www.creativeimpressions.com

Daisy D's Paper Co.
(888) 601-8955
www.daisydspaper.com

Delta/Rubber Stampede
(800) 423-4135
www.deltacrafts.com

Deluxe Designs
(480) 497-9005
www.deluxecuts.com

Design Originals
(800) 877-7820
www.d-originals.com

Diane's Daughters
(801) 621-8392
www.dianesdaughters.com

Die Cuts With A View
(801) 224-6766
www.diecutswithaview.com

Doodlebug Design Inc.
(801) 952-0555
www.doodlebug.ws

Duncan Enterprises
(800) 438-6226
www.duncancrafts.com

DYMO Corp.
global.dymo.com

Eclectic
(800) 693-4667
www.eclecticproducts.com

EK Success Ltd.
(800) 524-1349
www.eksuccess.com

Emagination Crafts
(866) 238-9770
www.emaginationcrafts.com

Epson America Inc.
(800) 338-2349
www.epson.com

Fiskars Brands Inc.
(866) 348-5661
www.fiskars.com

Fontwerks
(604) 942-3105
www.fontwerks.com

Gin-X/Imagination Project
(888) 477-6532
www.imaginationproject.com

Glue Dots International
(262) 814-8500
www.gluedots.com

Golden Artist Colors Inc.
(800) 959-6543
www.goldenpaints.com

Gorilla Glue
(800) 966-3458
www.gorillaglue.com

Grassroots
(262) 695-6429
www.grassrootscreative.com

Great Impressions
(800) 373-5908
www.greatimpressionsstamps.com

Green Sneakers Inc.
(908) 766-2181
www.greensneakers.com

Harbor Freight
(843) 676-2603
www.harborfreight.com

Heidi Swapp/Advantus Corp.
(904) 482-0092
www.heidiswapp.com

Hero Arts Rubber Stamps
(800) 822-4376
www.heroarts.com

Hewlett-Packard Co.
(800) 477-5010
www.hp.com

Jacquard Products: Rupert, Gibbon & Spider Inc.
(800) 442-0455
www.jacquardproducts.com

Jeneva & Co.
www.jenevaandcompany.com

Jesse James & Co. Inc./ Dress It Up
(610) 435-7899
www.dressitup.com

JudiKins
(310) 515-1115
www.judikins.com

Junkitz
(732) 792-1108
www.junkitz.com

K&Company
(888) 244-2083
www.kandcompany.com

Kandi Corp.
(800) 985-2634
www.kandicorp.com

Karen Foster Design
(801) 451-1373
www.scrapbookpaper.com

KI Memories
(972) 243-5595
www.kimemories.com

Kreinik Mfg. Co. Inc.
(800) 537-2166
www.kreinik.com

Krylon/Sherwin-Williams Co.
(800) 4KRYLON
www.krylon.com

LazerLetterz
www.lazerletterz.com

Leave Memories
www.leavememories.com

Li'l Davis Designs
www.lildavisdesigns.com

LuminArte Inc.
(866) 229-1544
www.luminarteinc.com

Magic Scraps
(904) 482-0092
www.magicscraps.com

Making Memories
(801) 294-0430
www.makingmemories.com

Mark Richards Enterprises Inc.
(888) 901-0091
www.markrichardsusa.com

McGill Inc.
(800) 982-9884
www.mcgillinc.com

me & my BIG ideas
www.meandmybigideas.com

Melissa Frances/ Heart & Home Inc.
(905) 686-9031
www.melissafrances.com

Memories Complete
(801) 492-1992
www.memoriescomplete.com

Mrs. Grossman's
(800) 429-4549
www.mrsgrossmans.com

Mrs. O'Leary's/Artful Illusions
(316) 262-0600
www.mrsolearys.com

My Mind's Eye Inc.
(801) 298-3709
www.mymindseyeinc.com

Nunn Designs
mail-order source:
My Daughter's Wish
(925) 952-4437
www.mydaughterswish.com

Paper Adventures
(414) 645-5760
www.paperadventures.com

The Paper Co.
www.ancrestwood.com

Paper House Productions
(800) 255-7316
www.paperhouseproductions.com

The Paper Loft
(951) 551-5870
www.paperloft.com

Paper Salon
(800) 627-2648
www.papersalon.com

The Paper Studio
www.paperstudio.com.au

Pebbles Inc.
www.pebblesinc.com

Pennywise Arts
www.pennywisearts.com

Plaid/All Night Media
(800) 842-4197
www.plaidonline.com

Postmodern Designs
(405) 321-3176

Prima Marketing Inc.
(909) 627-5532
www.primamarketinginc.com

Provo Craft
mail-order source:
Creative Express
(800) 563-8679
www.creativexpress.com

The Punch Bunch
(254) 791-4209
www.thepunchbunch.com

Queen & Co.
www.queenandco.com

QuicKutz Inc.
(801) 765-1144
www.quickutz.com

Ranger Industries Inc.
(732) 389-3535
www.rangerink.com

RubberStamp Ave.
(541) 665-9981
www.RubberStampAve.com

Rubbernecker Stamp Co.
(909) 673-0747
www.rubbernecker.com

Rusty Pickle
(801) 746-1045
www.rustypickle.com

Sakura Hobby Craft Inc.
(310) 212-7878
www.sakuracraft.com

Scenic Route Paper Co.
(801) 785-0761
www.scenicroutepaper.com

Scrapworks
(801) 363-1010
www.scrapworks.com

SEI
(800) 333-3279
www.shopsei.com

Sizzix/Ellison
(877) 355-4766
www.sizzix.com

Stampendous
(800) 869-0474
www.stampendous.com

Stampin' Up!
(800)-STAMPUP
www.stampinup.com

Stampington & Co.
(877) STAMPER
www.stampington.com

Stamp Francisco
(360) 210-4031
www.stampfrancisco

Sticker Studio
www.stickerstudio.com

Strathmore Artist Paper
(800) 353-0375
www.strathmoreartist.com

Technique Tuesday
www.techniquetuesday.com

Therm O Web
(847) 520-5200
www.thermoweb.com

Tsukineko Inc.
(800) 769-6633
www.tsukineko.com

Uchida of America
(800) 541-5877
www.uchida.com

USArtquest Inc.
(800) 200-7848
www.usartquest.com

Walnut Hollow
(800) 950-5101
www.walnuthollow.com

The Warm Co.
(800) 234-WARM
www.warmcompany.com

Westrim Crafts
(800) 727-2727
www.westrimcrafts.com

DESIGNER INDEX

INDEX

PHOTO BOOKS, JOURNALS & ALBUMS

ALTERED ART: BOOKS, CDS, TINS

HOME DECOR

CARDS & TAGS

UNIQUE MEMORY DISPLAYS

FRAMES

"Seeking" on page 97